BIRTH WITHOUT VIOLENCE

BIRTH WITHOUT VIOLENCE

FREDERICK LEBOYER

ALFRED A. KNOPF NEW YORK 1980

This is a Borzoi Book published by Alfred A. Knopf, Inc.

Translation Copyright © 1975 by Alfred A. Knopf, Inc.

All rights reserved under International and Pan-American Copyright Conventions.

Published in the United States by Alfred A. Knopf, Inc., New York,

and simultaneously in Canada by Random House of Canada Limited, Toronto.

Distributed by Random House, Inc., New York.

Originally published in France as Pour Une Naissance Sans Violence

by Editions du Seuil, Paris. Copyright © 1974 by Editions du Seuil.

ISBN:0-394-49581-0

Library of Congress Catalog Card Number: 74-21293

Manufactured in the United States of America

Published March 31, 1975

Reprinted Ten Times

Twelfth Printing, April 1980

All the photographs were taken by Frederick Lebover and Pierre-Marie Goulet

except for those on pages 11, 13, and 23, which were supplied by I. M. S. Stockholm.

BIRTH WITHOUT VIOLENCE

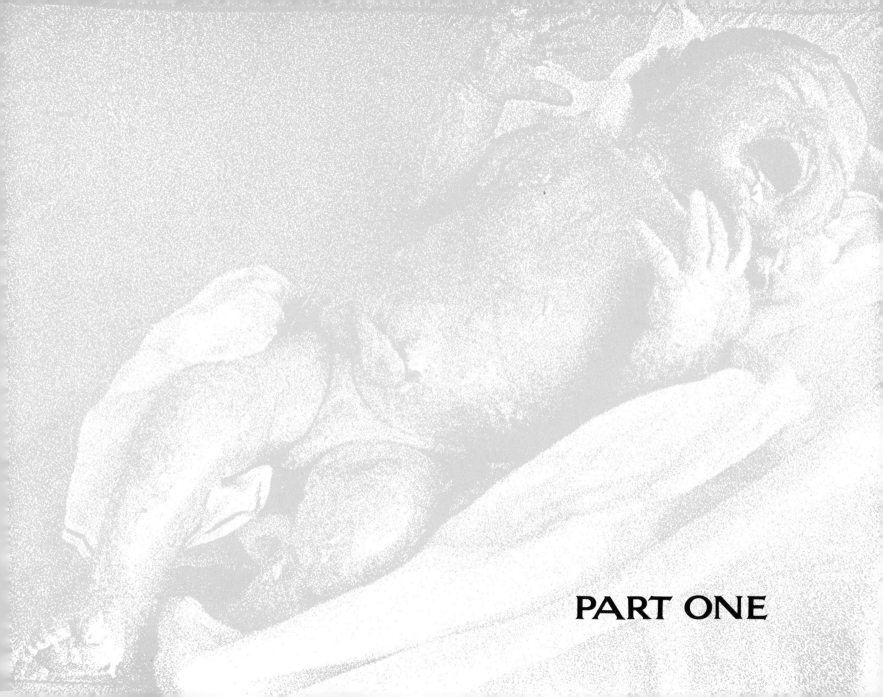

PART ONE

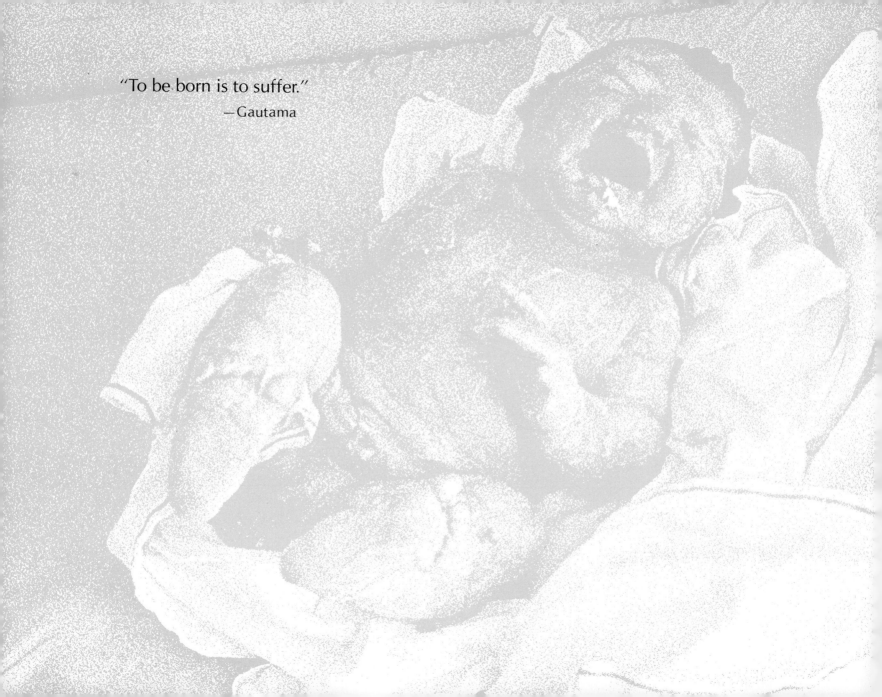

"To be born is to suffer."
—Gautama

"Do you believe that birth is an enjoyable experience—for the baby?"

"Birth?...Enjoyable?"

"You heard me....Do you believe that babies feel happy coming into this world?"

"You're joking."

"Why should I be joking?"

"Because babies are just babies."

"What is that supposed to mean?"

"That babies aren't capable of intense feeling."

"What makes you so certain?"

"Babies don't have fully developed feelings."

"How do you *know*?"

"Well, don't you agree?"

"If I did, I wouldn't be asking."

"But everybody knows they don't."

"Since when has that ever been a good reason to believe anything?"

"True. But newborn babies can't see or even hear, so how can they feel unhappy?"

"Even if they can't see or hear, that doesn't stop them from crying their hearts out."

"A baby has to test its lungs. That's common knowledge."

"Nonsense."

"Well, that's what people say."

"People say all kinds of stupid things. But do you really believe that babies feel nothing at all while they're being born?"

"Obviously they don't."

"I'm not so sure. After all, young children suffer overwhelming agonies about things that seem quite trivial to us—they feel a thousand times more intensely than we do."

"Yes, I know, but newborn babies are so tiny."

"What does size have to do with it?"

"Well..."

"And why do they scream so loud if they're not in some kind of pain or misery?"

"I don't know—a reflex I suppose. But I'm sure they're not feeling anything."

"But *why* aren't they?"

"Because they have no conscious awareness."

"Ah. So you think that means they have no soul."

"I don't know about the soul."

"But this consciousness...why is it so important?"

"Consciousness is the beginning of being a person."

"Are you trying to tell me that babies aren't fully human because they're not fully conscious? Tell me more...."

2

How many times have I heard that kind of discussion. It leads nowhere.

Things are simple. It's we who complicate them.

When children come into the world, the first thing they do is cry. And everyone rejoices.

"My baby's crying!" the mother exclaims happily, astonished that something so small can make so much noise.

And how does everyone else react?

The reflexes are normal. The machine works.

But are we machines?

Aren't cries always an expression of pain?

Isn't it conceivable that the baby is in anguish?

What makes us assume that birth is less painful for the child than it is for the mother?

And if it is, does anyone care?

No one, I'm afraid, judging by how little attention we pay to a baby when it arrives.

What a tragedy that we're all so determined to believe that this "thing" can't hear, can't see, can't *feel*...

So how could "it" feel pain?

"It" cries, "it" howls. So?

In short, "it" is an object.

But what if "it" is already a *person*?

3

Already a person! That is a contradiction of everything we believe.

Common sense suggests we begin by looking at the facts.

Which tell us absolutely nothing.

Because babies can't actually "tell" us anything. They don't speak in words.

Nor do porpoises. Or birds. But that doesn't prevent *them* from communicating.

Are there languages without words? Of course. We know there are, only our vanity keeps us from acknowledging them.

Just watch someone accidentally swallow something boiling hot, and you see how eloquently he speaks—without words!

He leaps up, hops from foot to foot, frantically waves his hands. His face is contorted, his eyes are watering. Whether he is from Moscow, Mombasa, or Miami, he's managed to say, "I've burned myself"—and say it without using a single word.

And compared to being born, burning your throat is nothing at all. If there's one thing a newborn baby doesn't lack, it's the ability to express itself.

Newborn babies don't talk?

Let's wait a moment before making up our minds.

4

What more proof do we need?

That tragic expression, those tight-shut eyes, those twitching eyebrows...

That howling mouth, that squirming head trying desperately to find refuge...

Those hands stretching out to us, imploring, begging, then retreating to shield the face—that gesture of dread.

Those furiously kicking feet, those arms that suddenly pull downward to protect the stomach.

The flesh that is one great shudder.

This baby is not speaking?

Every inch of the body is crying out: "Don't touch me!"

And at the same time pleading: "Don't leave me! Help me!"

Has there ever been a more heartrending appeal?

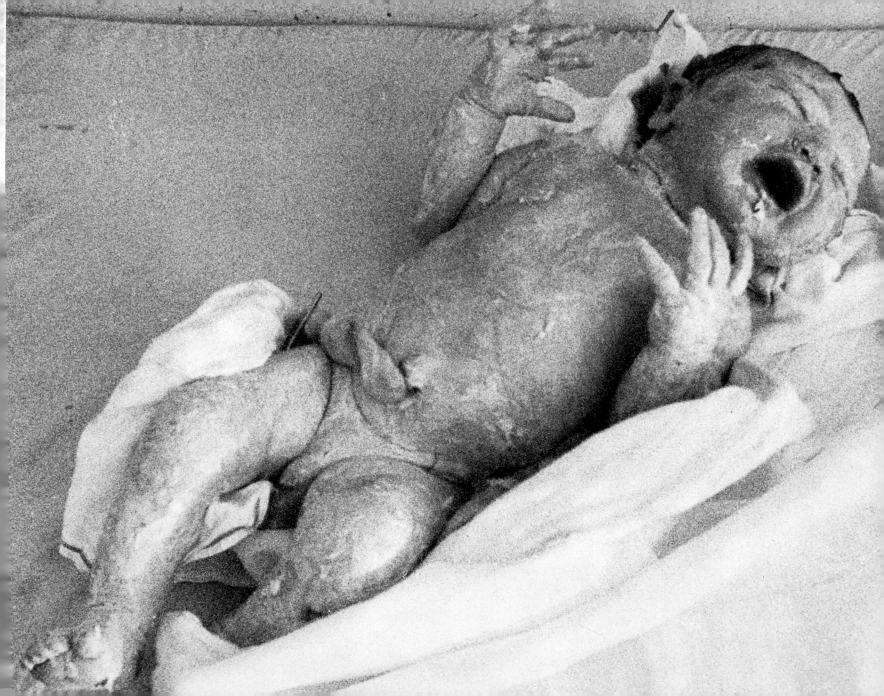

And yet this appeal—as old as birth itself—has been misunderstood, has been ignored, has simply gone unheard.

How can this have been? How can this still be?

A newborn baby doesn't speak?

No. It is we who do not listen.

5

And so we begin to wonder.

This little creature already a person?

Suffering? Howling with grief?

But it's so young, so small...

Again! Something in us resists, doesn't wish to hear, refuses to believe. We close our eyes, we guard our precious peace of mind.

Clearly we find it intolerable to look...to see...

Pictures of newborn infants are just not bearable. They could equally well be pictures of criminals who have undergone torture and are about to die.

People turn away and say: "No! I can't stand it."

Or: "Suffering? Do you really believe they are suffering?"

What you won't see can't hurt you.

Others try to argue: "But it isn't possible. Birth isn't like that, or we'd know about it. You're showing us an infant being tortured, a baby in the hands of sadists."

No. It's nothing like that.

It's only birth.

No monsters, no sadists. Just people like you and me. People whose minds are elsewhere.

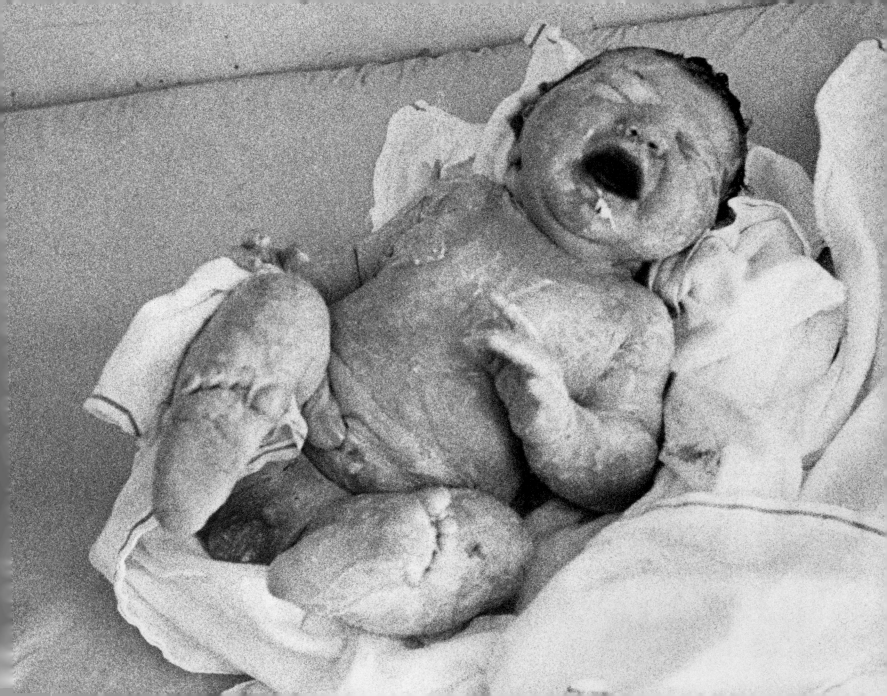

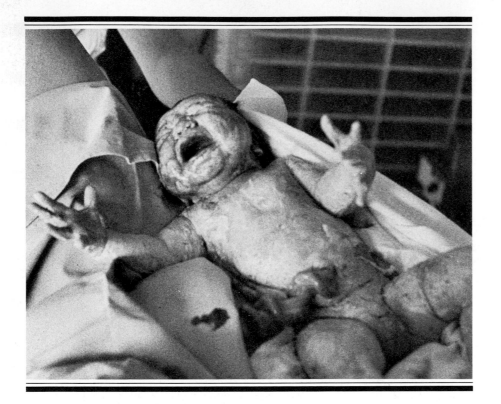

"They have eyes but do not see."

Blind men and women whose eyes are wide open. Do you want to watch them at it?

Watch.

6

A small creature has just been born. The father and mother gaze at it with delight. The young practitioner shares their joy.

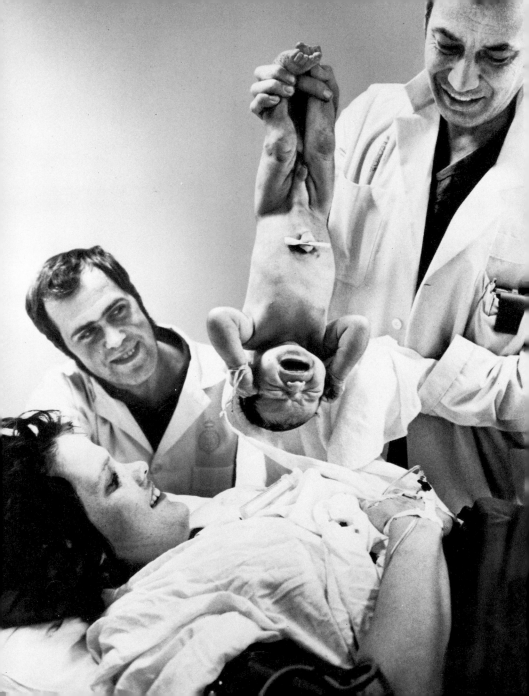

One dazzling smile lights up all their faces. They radiate happiness.

All of them, that is, except the child.

The child?

Oh, dear God, it can't be true!

This mask of agony, of horror. These hands—above all, these hands—clasping the head...

This is the gesture of someone struck by lightning. The gesture you see in the mortally wounded, the moment before they die.

Can birth hold so much suffering, so much pain? While the parents look on in ecstasy, oblivious.

No, we can't accept it.

And yet...it's true.

7

Why is the young doctor smiling, why does he look so pleased? Out of happiness for the child? Not really.

He's completed "his" delivery. He's succeeded at something that's not always so easy. The infant is there, crying loudly, as it's "supposed" to be. The mother is safe. Everything has turned out for the best.

The doctor smiles with relief. He is justifiably pleased...with *himself!*

What about the mother?

Radiant expression, ecstatic smile. But what is she smiling about? The beauty of her child? Not really.

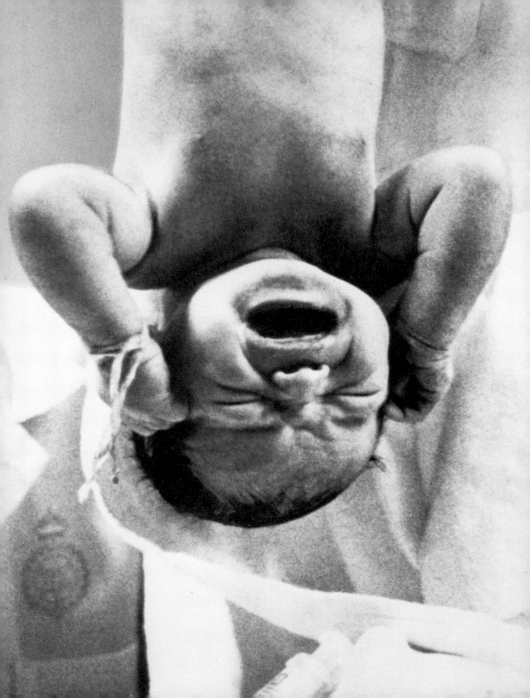

She's smiling because it's over.

She has completed "her" delivery without all the suffering she was dreading. She's amazed. And relieved. And—justifiably—proud of herself.

She's smiling with delight.

She's pleased...with *herself*.

And who can blame her?

Finally, what about the father?

A happy man. There will be a new generation...a baby who will grow up to reproduce, trait for trait, its father's perfections.

And finally, this man who may never before have truly created anything has created a child.

And so he is proud. And pleased. But pleased with *himself*.

Yes, everyone is pleased. With themselves.

As for the child...

8

Is there anything we can do?

Happily, there is some hope.

"You will give birth in pain," says the Bible.

But today a woman can give birth joyfully.

A miracle.

But how can she be joyful while her child is still being crucified? It cannot be.

Should the woman then renounce her joy?

No, certainly not.

We must simply now do for the child what we have already done for the mother. Or at least we must try.

9

Where can we begin?

The mother is being prepared for her almost painless delivery. But what can we do to prepare the child? And when? While it is still in the womb?

Are fine electrodes the answer, inserted into the tiny skull through the mother's stomach?

For God's sake, no. Although these days, technology is capable of such things.

But that is not *our* way.

We must begin by understanding.

Understanding *why* the newborn infant suffers so much.

The answer is contained in the question. And to ask "Why do babies suffer while being born?" is to open our ears at last to what they have been crying out so desperately for so long.

We must listen to them, we must try to hear, to understand.

And we will be halfway there.

10

What makes being born so frightful is the intensity, the boundless scope and variety of the experience, its suffocating richness.

People say—and believe—that a newborn baby feels nothing. He feels *everything*.

Everything—utterly, without choice or filter or discrimination.

Birth is a tidal wave of sensation, surpassing anything we can imagine. A sensory experience so vast we can barely conceive of it.

The baby's senses are at work. Totally.

They are sharp and open—new.

What are our senses compared to theirs?

And the sensations of birth are rendered still more intense by contrast with what life was like before. (Yes—the senses were already at work long before the baby was here, among us, in our world.)

Admittedly, these sensations are not yet organized into integrated, coherent perceptions. Which makes them all the stronger, all the more violent, unbearable—literally maddening.

11

Let us begin with sight.

It is claimed that a newborn infant is blind.

Judging by the abundance of blinding lights that are used during deliveries everywhere, this must be a universal postulate.

Don't they aim lamps and floodlights at the new arrival?

Of course. Who would dim lights for a blind man?

These lights are certainly convenient for the attending physician.

But what about the baby?

When the infant's head is barely out of its mother's genital passage, while its body is still captive, you see the eyes opening. And shutting. Immediately, violently. The tiny face presents an indescribable picture of suffering, and the familiar cry bursts out.

If "seeing" means being able to construct mental images out of what the eyes are exposed to, then no, the newborn infant doesn't see. Not yet.

But if seeing is perceiving light, then yes, the infant does see. Vividly.

The baby has the same love, the same thirst, for the light that plants and flowers have.

The baby is mad for this light, drunk with it. So much so that we should take infinite precautions; we should offer it infinitely slowly.

In fact, the baby is so sensitive to light that he or she perceives it while still in the mother's womb.

If a woman more than six months pregnant is naked in the sunlight, the infant within her sees it as a golden haze.

And now this little creature, so sensitive to the light, is thrust suddenly out of its dark cavern. And its eyes are exposed to flood-lights!

The infant howls aloud. And why should this surprise us? Its eyes have just been burned.

Would we *choose* to drive an infant mad with pain?

The poor little child squeezes its eyes shut. But what help is the fragile, transparent barrier of its eyelids?

They say a newborn child is blind?

No, it is *blinded*.

12

And what about hearing? Is the baby deaf?

No more than blind.

By the time babies are actually born, their ears have already been serving them for a long time.

While they are still in the womb, the noises of their mothers' bodies reach them: joints cracking, intestinal rumblings. And giving the rhythm to it all is the strong drumbeat of the mother's heart.

And then—her voice. The mother's voice, which sets its stamp on the child forever.

Each voice is unique, inimitable—the way fingerprints are.

The unborn baby is marked by its mother's voice, its nuances, its inflections, its moods.

And this is not all.

Just as they perceive the light, unborn infants perceive the sounds of the world—despite the thickness of the mother's stomach wall.

They receive them the way fish do, through the waters in which they bathe. Sounds modulated, transformed.

And then birth!

Sounds—muted until now—suddenly strike the young arrival with all their force. The waters have vanished; the protective shield of the mother's stomach is gone.

The young ears are suddenly vulnerable. Nothing protects them any longer from the world's uproar.

The infant is born into a thunderous explosion. It convulses. Should we be surprised?

The world cries out. The child gives an answering cry.

Once again, it is we who are deaf.

How can we know what a child is hearing as it is born?

Who bothers to lower his voice in the delivery room? There is more shouting than speaking.

"Come on! Push, push! Again, again!"

And in the general excitement when the child emerges, more exclamations, new explosions of sound.

How does the infant react?

Again, by cradling its head in its hands.

The newborn infant deaf?

No.

13

Poor little creature! What a fate, to be born and to fall into our hands, victim of our ignorance and cruelty!

It has been blinded and deafened.

What about its sense of touch?

Its skin—thin, fine, almost without a protective surface layer—is as exposed and raw as tissue that has suffered a burn. The slightest touch makes it quiver.

An infant even trembles when someone comes near it.

Until birth, its skin knew only the velvet caress of membrane. Then, suddenly, it is wrapped in harsh fabrics.

Newborn babies arrive in our world as if on a carpet of thorns.

They'll adapt to it.

By withdrawing into themselves, by deadening their senses.

But when they first land on these thorns, they howl.

Naturally.

And idiots that we are, we laugh.

14

And all this is only the beginning.

Yes, this hell exists. And burns. It is not a fable.

This hell does not come at the end of our life.

It is here. At the beginning.

Hell is what the infant must suffer through to arrive here among us.

Its flames assail the child from every direction; they burn the eyes, the skin, penetrate down through the flesh; they devour.

This fire is what the infant feels as the air rushes into the lungs.

The air, which enters and sweeps through the trachea, and expands the alveoli, is like acid poured on a wound.

This is no exaggeration. We have only to watch someone trying to inhale cigarette smoke for the first time. It's nothing to the habitual smoker—his saturated membranes have long ago given up the battle. But the novice, whose tissues are still reasonably undamaged, no sooner takes a lungful of smoke than he explodes in a frantic effort to be rid of its intolerable burning. His eyes water, his face turns crimson.

Or imagine a child who, fooled by the colorlessness of pure alcohol, accidentally drinks it in place of water. No sooner does it reach the child's throat than it is vomited back up in a single violent reaction, while tears mix with his trembling hiccups, and he flushes scarlet.

For the infant coming into this world, the burning sensation of air entering the lungs surpasses every other horror.

Seared to its very depths, the entire body quivers, shudders with horror, protests.

Everything struggles to repulse the enemy.

And this is the baby's cry!

The cry that marks and celebrates the passage into life.

This is a "No!" A passionate, violent protest. A cry that is as desperate as it is useless, since this thing "must be."

For it is only the first of all the breaths that are to follow—and each burns more than the one before.

15

And is *this* all?

Alas, no.

When the infant emerges, the doctor seizes it by one foot and holds it dangling, head down.

As usual, his intentions are good.

The infant's body is, in fact, quite slippery, coated as it is with *vernix caseosa*, the thick, white grease that covers it from head to toe. The infant is held by the foot to prevent it from slipping and falling. Such a handhold is sure. Convenient.

Convenient for *us*.

And for the infant?

What does it feel, finding itself suddenly upside down?

Indescribable vertigo.

Those who have had nightmares in which they plunge suddenly into a void are familiar with this sensation. It stems directly from this moment during their birth.

To understand the full horror of such a fall into the abyss, it is essential that we go back for a moment to the mother's womb.

We know very little about our bodies, so little that we forget the importance of the spine.

It is "behind" us. Yet it rules our every mood—whether vibrant and gay, lethargic and sad.

Strength is "in the back," fear "between the shoulder blades." Our states of mind are really the states of our back! And to understand the horror of the shock we inflict on an infant when we suspend it by its feet, we must first realize what the back is undergoing at that moment. To measure the difference between its "before" and its "now."

"Before" was what the backbone experienced when, with great difficulty, the infant was trying to find its way into the world.

In fact, we must return even further, return into the mother's uterus. And there we must relive what this "spine" has undergone.

16

A baby's life passes through two stages in the womb: two seasons of equal duration, which oppose each other like winter and summer.

The first is "the Golden Age."

The embryonic stage, when the infant is like a small plant, growing and blossoming.

Anchored.

The embryo becomes the fetus; the plant becomes animal. Movement comes to it, beginning at the trunk, spreading outward to the extremities.

The fetus stirs, takes pleasure in its limbs. And in its freedom.

Supported by waters all around it, the fetus is weightless, light as a bird, agile and lively as a fish.

Its contentment and freedom are limitless. As is its kingdom, whose boundaries it brushes against from time to time.

For in this first half of pregnancy, the egg (the membrane which contains the fetus and the fluids in which it is bathed) grows more rapidly than the child.

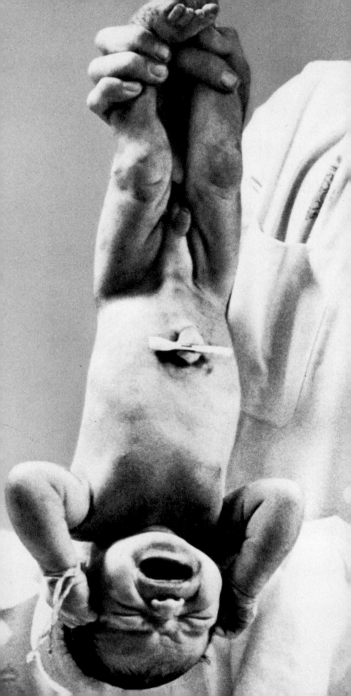

Fast as the infant develops, its kingdom grows faster. So the baby never suffers a sense of confinement.

Yes, its contentment is unlimited. And the photographs we have of it at this stage show a completely relaxed expression.

A vision of serenity.

This is the Golden Age.

But it doesn't last.

In the depths of the womb, the infant has been overtaken by Natural Law. The law of universal revolution, which stipulates that everything must become its opposite.

Midway through the pregnancy, everything changes. The infant continues to grow and to develop rapidly. But the egg that contains him grows only slightly by comparison.

His tribulations begin.

The baby begins to feel closed in; slowly the universe is contracting.

What was once unbounded space becomes more confining each day. Gone is the limitless ocean of earlier—and happier—days; that absolute freedom is no more.

And one day the baby finds itself…a prisoner.

And in such a prison!

The cell so small that the prisoner's body touches the walls—all of them—at once. Walls that draw nearer all the time. To the point when one day, the infant's back and the mother's uterus seem to be fused together.

For a long time, the little creature won't accept it. Struggles. Protests.

In vain. Inexorably the prison closes in.

The child accepts—is there any choice?

The spine curls up, the head bends, the whole body makes itself small.

Perhaps some instinct suggests that none of this is permanent, that good can come from misfortune.

Each day the baby grows larger inside the shrinking prison.

And huddles up. Crouches. Submits.

Then one day the prison comes to life. No longer merely to keep the infant huddled in submission, it begins, like some octopus, to hug and crush.

Terrified, the infant endures it.

The contraction ceases, returns, goes away again...then there is another. Not strong; playful.

So that once the infant has recovered from its initial fright, it comes to like them.

To wait for the contractions, to hope for them.

When they come—embracing the infant, hugging it—it surrenders to them; arches its back, quivers with pleasure at this sensual game.

And these "caresses" are going to last a whole month—the ninth.

Painless for the mother, they prepare the child for the contractions of actual labor, which will be ten times more intense.

17

One day, these contractions are no longer a game. They crush, they stifle, they assault.

One day labor starts. The delivery has begun.

An intransigent force—wild, out of control—has gripped the infant.

A blind force that hammers at it and impels it downward.

It is no longer enough for the infant to bend its back.

Overpowered, it huddles up as tightly as it can. With its head tucked in and its shoulders hunched together, it is hardly more than a little ball of fright.

The prison has gone berserk, demanding its prisoner's death. The walls close in still further. The cell becomes a passageway; the passage, a tunnel.

With its heart bursting, the infant sinks into this hell.

Its fear is without limit.

Then, suddenly, fear changes to anger.

Enraged, the infant hurls itself against the barrier. At all costs, it must break through. Free itself.

Yet all this force, this monstrous unremitting pressure that is crushing the baby, pushing it out toward the world—and this blind wall, which is holding it back, confining it—

These things are all one: the mother!

She is driving the baby out.

At the same time she is holding it in, preventing its passage.

It is *she* who is the enemy. She who stands between the child and life.

Only one of them can prevail; it is mortal combat.

The infant is like one possessed.

Mad with agony and misery, alone, abandoned, it fights with the strength of despair.

The monster drives the baby lower still. And not satisfied with crushing, it twists it in a refinement of cruelty. The infant's head and body execute a corkscrew motion to clear the narrow passage of the pelvis.

And the infant's head—bearing the brunt of the struggle until it is almost forced down between the shoulder blades, down onto the chest—why doesn't the head give way?

The baby is now at the height of its travail. The effort required is too great. The end is surely near. Death seems certain.

The monster bears down one more time, and it is then that...

18

Then that everything explodes!

The whole world bursts open.

No more tunnel, no prison, no monster.

The child is born.

And the barrier...? Disappeared, thrown away.

Nothing!—except the void, with all its horror.

Freedom!—and it is intolerable.

Where am I...?

Everything was pressing in on me, crushing me, but at least I had a form.

My mother, my hated prison—where are you?

Alone, I am nothingness, dizziness.

Take me back! Contain me again. Destroy me!

But let me exist...

19

The infant is crazed with pain. And for a simple reason: suddenly nothing is supporting his back.

And it is in this paroxysm of confusion, of despair and distress, that someone seizes the baby by a foot and suspends it over the void.

The spinal column has been strained, bent, pushed, and twisted to the limit of its endurance—and now it is robbed of all support.

And the head, so supremely involved in the passage outward— now it also is dangling, twisting.

And this at the very moment when, in order to calm this vast terror, this panic, what is essential is a coming together with the mother, a *reuniting*.

If our deliberate intention was to teach the child that it had fallen into an indifferent world, a world of ignorance, cruelty, and folly, what better course of action could we have chosen?

20

Now, on what surface do we place the terrified baby, who has so painfully emerged from the enveloping warmth and softness of the womb?

On a scale!

Often of steel—a cold that burns like fire.

The cries redouble.

And so does the joy of the onlookers.

Particularly if the baby's weight, when it is announced, is impressive.

"That's my baby crying!" the ecstatic mother says.

The baby is picked up again.

Again by the feet, head dangling.

Once again, vertigo.

Once again, terror.

The baby is laid down again.

On some corner of the table, on top of some cloth.

And abandoned. Still crying.

And is this all?

No, it is still necessary to attend to the eyes, to put drops in them.

The body struggles.

The eyes are forced open.

And several drops of burning liquid are squeezed in.

21

And now the infant is alone.

Abandoned by everyone and everything, lost in a world as hostile as it is incomprehensible. Still trembling with terror. Hiccuping, choking.

Unhappiness is so ingrained in most babies by this time that they can hope for nothing else.

If someone approaches, they tremble even more.

And then we see an extraordinary thing: when the tears and the gasping and the pain become too much, the infant flees.

Not literally; its legs, of course, cannot help it.

The baby disappears into itself.

Doubles up again.

Curls up into a ball.

Folds its arms and legs against itself.

And once again adopts the fetal position.

Symbolically, it has taken itself back into the womb.

Overcome by the horror of the world, it returns to paradise.

It objects to having been born. It becomes a fetus again.

And once again…a prisoner.

22

Calm.

But not for long.

The baby is picked up again. Dressed.

In things that are tight, rough, heavy—but which are so pretty! Which "go so well." Which please the mother, the family, their friends…

Once again the baby protests, bursts into loud sobs. Cries, howls.

For as long as its strength holds out.

And when it is no longer able to cry, it collapses.

Sinks into sleep.

Its only refuge.

Its only friend.

23

This is birth.

The torture of an innocent.

What futility to believe that so great a cataclysm will not leave its mark.

Its traces are everywhere—in the skin, in the bones, in the stomach, in the back.

In all our human folly.

In our madness, our tortures, our prisons.

In legends, epics, myths.

In the Scriptures.

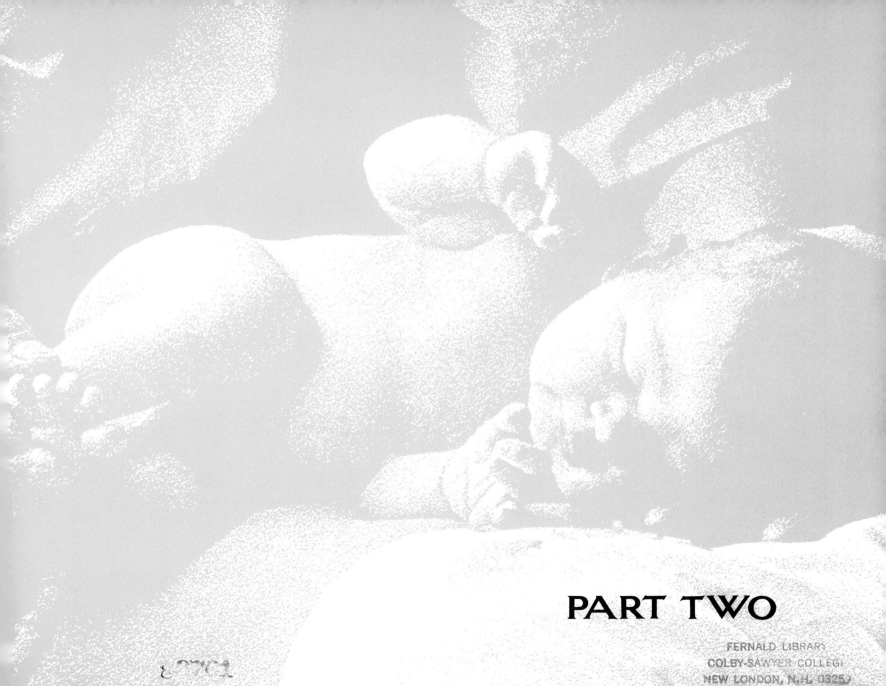

PART TWO

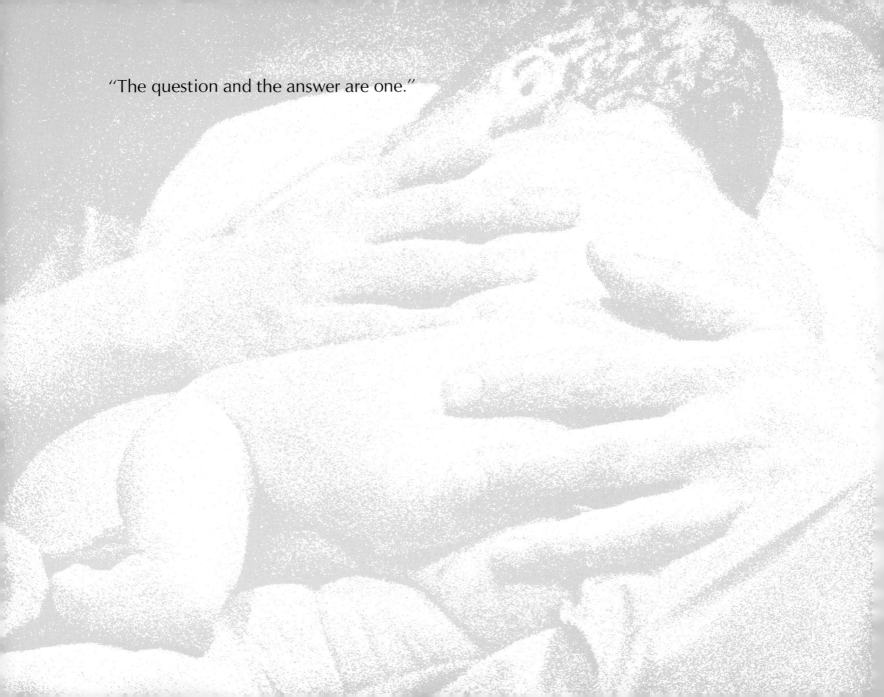

"The question and the answer are one."

All of this is terrifying, overwhelming; it leaves us almost without hope. Without hope for the child.

Should we prepare the infant while still in the womb? With fine electrodes?

No, it isn't the child who needs preparation. It is we ourselves.

If we manifest such blindness, so little understanding in the way we welcome newborn children, can we marvel that the world is…the way it is?

But let us concentrate on specifics of birth itself. Let us see how even a modest increase of sensitivity on our part can make an immense difference.

2

There is a disquieting paradox in birth.

The child suddenly finds itself liberated from an unendurable captivity…and weeps!

This also happens, so they say, to prisoners who are suddenly set free.

The liberty they have dreamt of so long intoxicates them—and panics them.

They begin to miss their prison bars. Both better off and worse off than before, unconsciously they behave in ways that will ensure them reimprisonment.

In the same way, the infant—suddenly liberated—howls.

We want to cry out, "But this is absurd! Why are you crying when you should be exulting? Now at last you can stretch, reach

35

out, kick, wave your arms in the air. And yet you are crying! Look around you. Realize what has happened to you. Recognize your happiness."

Why won't the baby understand? Listen to reason?

Reason? In a tiny creature only a few minutes old? Then what *can* we tell the baby?

"Tell" is not the right word.

The baby should be addressed in its *own* language. The language that precedes words.

Are we, then, to speak in gestures, as we would to a foreigner? Of course not.

We must go back still further and rediscover the universal language. Which is simply the language of love.

Speak of love to a newborn baby?

Yes, speak of love. Speak the language of lovers.

And what is the essential language of lovers?

Not speech. Touch.

Lovers are shy, modest. When they want to embrace, they seek the darkness; they turn out the light. Or simply close their eyes.

They create night for themselves. Touch becomes everything.

And in this darkness, they quiver, caress each other, lightly stroke each other.

Put their arms around each other.

Melt into well-being again, as in that ancient prison, the womb.

They are silent—words would be superfluous.

If there is any sound, it is a sigh of pleasure.

It is their hands that speak.

And their bodies listen and understand.

This is what newborn babies must have. This is how we should speak to them, how they can understand. Simply by tenderness, by touch.

Let us advance step by step, hoping to learn what we must do so as not to terrify the child who has come among us.

3

It is really quite simple.

Let us begin with the problem of sight.

And place ourselves, like lovers, in darkness.

Now our alertness, our sense of touch, grow keener. But, above all, this way the infant's eyes are spared.

Of course some light is necessary to watch over the mother, so that she will not be injured when the child's head emerges. But lamps and floodlights are unnecessary.

As soon as the head appears and the danger has passed, extinguish all the lights, except a small night light. It will be enough.

In the darkness, the mother will be able to make out her child's features only faintly. And this is all to the good, since newborn infants are almost always ugly, their features deformed by fear.

It is better that the mother discover her child by touching it. Better to feel before she sees. Better to sense this warm and trembling life, to be moved in her heart by what her *hands* tell her. To hold her child rather than merely look at it.

Later she will have plenty of time for that, when its face has relaxed into its true features.

This is the moment for her to speak to her baby quietly, to calm it with her touch.

Both of them, mother and child, have everything to gain by first meeting in the semidarkness.

But it is the child who benefits most, the child whose eyes are spared from the burning light.

4

As for hearing...

Nothing could be simpler: be silent.

Easy? Less so than it might seem.

By nature we're talkers. Even when our lips are still, the interior monologue does not slow down.

Besides, to be silent in someone else's company is so unsettling that we rarely attempt it.

To be silent, attentive, to *listen*, to hear that which is unspoken —all this demands great effort.

It is necessary to prepare oneself for this, to train oneself.

And to understand the why of it.

The first women whose babies were delivered in a silent room were so disturbed that their story is worth telling.

We were already talking very little—and in muted voices by the time each woman's labor was coming to an end. Thus there was hardly a sound in the room. And when the children were born, we did not speak a single word.

If occasionally it was absolutely necessary to say something —to give an order or make a suggestion—it was done in an all but inaudible whisper, so as not to disturb each child's first moments.

This procedure—completely natural—was surprisingly so disconcerting to the mothers that they quickly became panic-stricken.

Instead of continuously howling as expected, each baby merely uttered two or three healthy cries and then began its steady breathing. With the result that in the intense silence, what each woman heard...was the very absence of her baby's cry. Her eyes soon betrayed first surprise and then alarm, darting questioningly from one of us to the next.

Suddenly, unable to restrain what was in her heart, each burst out: "Why isn't my baby crying?" It was agonizing, astounding, heartbreaking: "Why isn't my baby crying?"

The surprise, the regret, the *accusation* in those questions dumfounded us. How deeply ingrained is the assumption that the newborn child must cry, how profound the unconscious acceptance that birth and suffering are one.

What could we say? How could we respond?

These women had not been sufficiently alerted or prepared for the silence.

We have come so far from the natural life that something as true and simple as this peacefulness can surprise and distress us.

"My baby's dead," each agonized voice continued.

"Your child is doing wonderfully," we said, motioning to her to lower her voice in order to spare the infant's ears.

Our whispering would upset her still more.

"Dead! My baby's dead!"

Dead? Her child was lying on her stomach—moving, stirring.

"Dead children are completely still. Feel your baby moving. Feel how happy he is!" All this said quietly.

How can we please both the mother and the child?

And then we tried, much too late, to explain the reason for our silence—our respect for the newborn child and its delicate hearing, our determination not to frighten it with the loudness of our voices. We tried to explain to these mothers that crying and suffering are not essential to birth. But our explanations failed to convince; their eyes were still full of doubt and sorrow.

Finally they grew calmer.

"Your baby is really doing splendidly, as well as a baby can," we said encouragingly.

"Do you really mean it?"

To be fair, we must admit that a newborn infant who begins gurgling happily after just a cry or two—who yawns and stretches, who enters life the way we awake from a restless sleep—is something of a surprise. It is as unexpected, as startling to those not accustomed to the idea as is a mother who gives birth smiling, without crying out, radiantly.

All of which is to say that we must prepare ourselves for this. We must be awake and aware.

Aware that the baby can hear, aware of how sensitive its hearing is, and how easily harmed.

In brief, we must all learn in this first moment to love the baby for itself. Not for ourselves.

That a child is a life entrusted to us all.

Mothers must let themselves feel, "I am a *mother*," and not, "This is *my child*."

Between the two there is a world of difference.

The future of the child.

5

This apprenticeship of silence—so indispensable for mothers—is just as important for those who perform the delivery: the obstetricians, the attendants.

People speak loudly in the delivery room. The calls to "push, push" are rarely whispered.

So profoundly wrong.

These loud outbursts upset the mother more than help her. Lowered voices can relax her. And do far more for her than shouting.

Those who assist in deliveries must learn this new silence. They too must be prepared to receive the child with care and respect.

6

Near-darkness...silence...

A profound peace steals over everything, almost unnoticed.

People don't raise their voices in church. On the contrary, instinctively, they lower them. And this too is a sacred place.

Darkness and quiet; what more is needed?

Patience. Or more accurately, the learning of an extreme slowness that comes close to immobility.

Without acceptance of this slowness, success is impossible; without it, we cannot truly communicate with an infant.

Relaxing, accepting the slow pace, letting it take command—all this requires training. As much for the mother as for those of us who attend her.

Success depends on our understanding, once again, from what a strange otherworld the baby has come to this one of ours.

We must remember that descending into hell, the baby advanced centimeter by centimeter. And as his movements became more and more constricted, he dammed up greater and greater force and energy.

Without experiencing this extreme slowness in our *own* bodies, it is impossible to understand birth. Impossible to receive the newborn baby properly.

His "time" is so slow as to approximate no movement at all.

Ours is an agitation bordering on frenzy.

Besides, we are never truly "here"—always "elsewhere." In the past, with our memories; in the future, with our plans. Always "before" or "after." Never *now*.

But we must learn to be "here."

To forget the future, to forget the past.

Once again, everything is very simple. And yet so hard to achieve.

How is it to be accomplished?

Only with the most passionate attention.

We who are watching must rediscover the newborn baby, as if this were the first baby we have ever seen. We must be so astounded…that we forget everything else. Ourselves included.

We must disappear.

So that only the baby remains.

We must look at this baby. Or better yet, be absorbed into its very being. Without complication. Without prejudice. In all innocence. All newness.

Become…this new person.

But we are looking too far ahead.

Let us wait for the baby.

7

Now.

Everything is ready. Darkness. Silence. Ourselves. Time stands still.

The child can make its entrance.

8

Now is the moment.

The baby emerges...first the head, and then the arms; we help to free them by sliding a finger under each armpit. Supporting the baby in this way, we lift the little body up, as if pulling someone out of the well. We *never* touch the head. And we settle the child immediately on its mother's belly.

What better place could there be? Her belly has the infant's exact shape and dimensions. Swelling a moment before, hollow now, the belly seems to lie there waiting, like a nest.

And its warmth and suppleness as it rises and falls with the rhythm of her breathing, its softness, the glowing life of its skin, all work together to create the best possible resting place for the child.

Finally—and this is crucial—the very closeness of contact permits the umbilical cord to be left intact.

9

To sever the umbilicus when the child has scarcely left the mother's womb is an act of cruelty whose ill effects are immeasurable. To conserve it intact while it still pulses is to transform the act of birth.

First, this forces the physician to be patient; it is an invitation to both the doctor and the mother to respect the baby's own life-rhythm.

And it does more.

When air rushes into the baby's lungs, it feels like burning fire.

Before he was born, the infant made no distinction between the world and himself, since "outside" and "inside" were all one. He knew nothing of the tension of opposites—nothing was cold, since cold can only be known by contrast with what is warm. An infant's body temperature and its mother's are always identical; how could there be any separation between them?

For the newborn infant to enter our world is to enter a universe of opposites, where everything is good or bad, pleasant or unpleasant, dry or wet…it is to discover these contradictions that cannot exist apart from one another.

And how does the infant enter this kingdom of opposites?

Through breathing. In taking its first breath, it crosses a threshold. And it is here.

The baby takes a breath. And from this inhalation springs its opposite—exhalation. Which in its turn…

A pendulum has been released into perpetual motion—the very principle of our world, where everything is breathing, balancing; where everything, always, is born from its opposite—day from night,

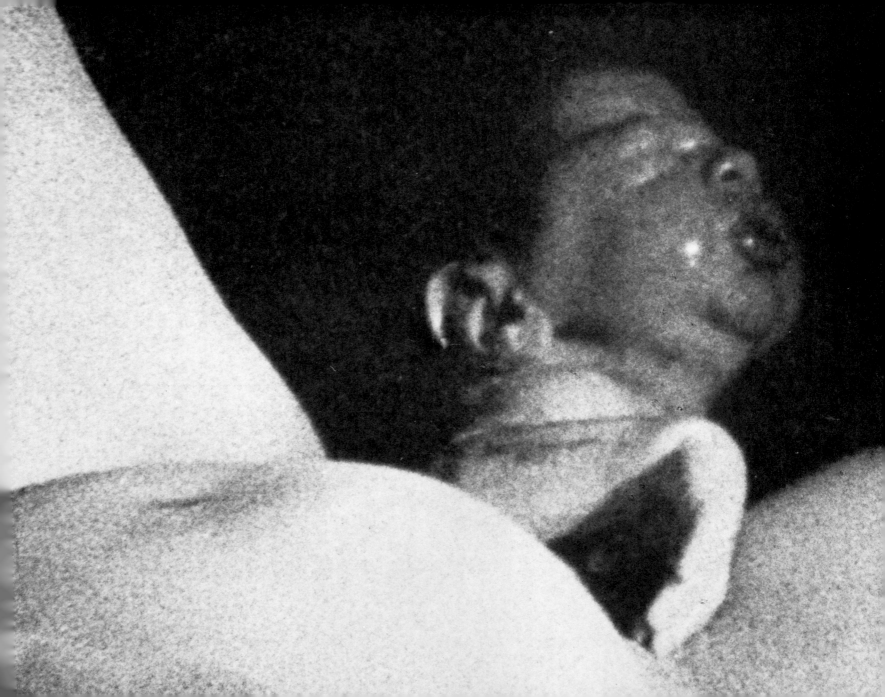

summer from winter, riches from poverty, strength from weakness.

Without end. Without beginning.

10

To breathe is to be in accord with creation, to be in harmony with the Universal, with its eternal motion.

More literally, it is to take in oxygen and to expel the wastes, essentially carbon dioxide.

But in this simple exchange, two worlds approach one another, attempt to touch, to mix, to meet: the world within and the world without.

Two worlds, separated now, try to recover each other, to become one again: the small "I" inside the vast world outside.

Into the lungs flow both the blood that rises from beneath, and the air that sweeps in from above.

Air and blood rush toward each other, eager to mix.

They are unable to do so, separated as they are by a wall, the thin partition of the alveoli.

And both "sigh" after their lost unity.

The blood arrives in the lungs—dull, depleted of oxygen, heavy with carbon dioxide and the other waste products that render it old, without vitality, exhausted. In the lungs it is going to shed its age, to recharge itself with youth and energy.

Transfigured by this passage into the Fountain of Youth, it departs—lively, rich, and red. Plunges down again to distribute its riches, rises again, burdened with wastes. Returns to the lungs, where it regenerates itself. And the circle continues indefinitely.

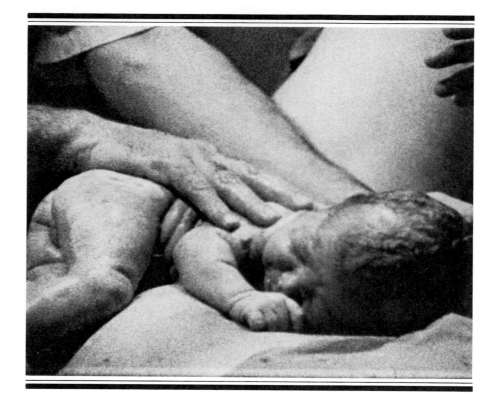

As for the heart, it is the prime mover, sending this regenerated blood to the thirsty tissues of the entire organism, along the course of what is called the major, or systemic, circulatory system. In an opposed but synchronous movement it draws the old, depleted blood back toward the source of renewal, the lungs. This is known as the minor, or pulmonary, circulatory system.

The minor circulatory system derives its name from the shortness of the journey the depleted blood makes from the heart to the lungs and back.

The major circulatory system is so-called because of the length of the trips the blood makes from the heart to the limits of its realm, the top of the head, the extremities of the limbs, the internal organs.

How do these things take place within the unborn fetus, whose lungs do not yet function?

The fetus's blood takes the same route ours does to regenerate itself.

It depends on the placenta to do this—the placenta functions as its lungs. The blood arrives there and leaves by way of the umbilical cord, which is nothing more than three tubes: a vein and two arteries in a sheath.

The blood regenerates itself in the placenta, not by contact with outside air but by contact with the mother's blood, which is restored in *her* lungs…in short: the mother breathes for her baby. Even as she eats for her baby, carries her baby, shelters her baby. Sleeps and dreams for her baby. Does everything for her baby.

Before this baby is born, dependence on the mother is total.

And what happens at birth? An extraordinary adventure, a vast change, a true revolution: the blood which until then has flowed through the umbilicus now ventures into the lungs!

The baby's blood abandons the old, familiar path, abandons the passage through the mother.

By breathing—by oxygenating its blood with its own lungs—the infant chooses the path of autonomy, of independence, of freedom.

Of course, this is only the first step. For everything but air the child still depends on its mother.

But the direction is what matters.

As for the blood, does it abruptly and rudely abandon the old route of the umbilicus-placenta all at once? Hurl itself like some mad thing into the lungs?

It all depends...this is really the essential question.

Depending on whether this transition occurs slowly, gently—or brutally, in panic and terror—birth becomes a peaceful awakening...or a tragic one.

11

Nature, they say, doesn't move forward in sudden leaps.

Yet birth is just such a leap forward. An exchange of worlds, of levels.

How can we resolve this contradiction? How does Nature make smooth a transition whose very essence is so violent?

Very simply.

Nature is a strict mother, but a loving one. We misunderstand her intentions; then we blame her for what follows.

Everything about birth is arranged so that both leap and landing are made as easy as possible.

The danger the child faces during birth has quite properly been stressed. This danger is anoxia: a deficiency of the precious oxygen to which the nervous system is so acutely sensitive.

If it happens that the child fails to receive oxygen, the result is irreparable damage to the brain: a person maimed for life.

So at all costs, the child must not lack oxygen at birth, not even for an instant.

As the experts tell us.

As Nature has always known.

She has arranged it so that during the dangerous passage of birth, the child is receiving oxygen from two sources rather than one: from the lungs *and* from the umbilicus.

Two systems functioning simultaneously, one relieving the other: the old one, the umbilicus, continues to supply oxygen to the baby until the new one, the lungs, has fully taken its place.

However, once the infant has been born and delivered from the mother, it remains bound to her by this umbilicus, which continues to beat for several long minutes: four...five...sometimes more.

Oxygenated by the umbilicus, sheltered from anoxia, the baby can settle into breathing without danger and without shock. At leisure. Without rush.

In addition, the blood has plenty of time to abandon its old route (which leads to the placenta) and progressively to fill the pulmonary circulatory system.

During this time, in parallel fashion, an orifice closes in the heart, which seals off the old route forever.

In short, for an average of four or five minutes, the newborn infant straddles two worlds. Drawing oxygen from two sources, it switches gradually from the one to the other, without a brutal transition. One scarcely hears a cry.

What is required for this miracle to take place? Only a little patience. Only a refusal to rush things. Only knowing enough to wait, giving the child time to adjust.

We can see that education is required; otherwise, how can we bear to wait five long minutes doing absolutely nothing? When *everything* inclines us to act: our mental laziness, our automatic assumptions, our habits. And our everlasting impatience.

12

For the baby, it makes an enormous difference.

Whether we cut the umbilical cord immediately or not changes everything about the way respiration comes to the baby, even conditions the baby's taste for life.

If the cord is severed as soon as the baby is born, this brutally deprives the brain of oxygen.

The alarm system thus alerted, the baby's entire organism reacts. Respiration is thrown into high gear as a response to aggression.

Everything in the body-language of the infant—in the frenzied agitation of its limbs, in the very tone of its cries—shows the immensity of its panic and its efforts to escape.

Entering life, what the baby meets is death. And to escape this death it hurls itself into respiration. The act of breathing, for a newborn baby, is a desperate last resort. Already the first conditioned reflex has been implanted, a reflex in which breathing and anguish will be associated forever. What a welcome into this world!

13

How do things unfold when we refrain from interfering, when we protect the umbilicus?

Doubly supplied with oxygen, the baby's brain is never threatened, even for a minute. Nothing occurs to set off the alarm system. Consequently, no attack, no anoxia, no panic or anguish.

Rather, a slow and gradual progression from one state to another...the blood changes course without sudden disruption.

The lungs are not convulsed into action.

When the infant emerges, it utters a cry. This is because the thorax—which until now has been constricted by external pressure —is suddenly relaxed and opens wide.

A void is created. The air rushes in. It is the first breath. A passive acceptance.

It is also a burning.

Wounded, the child responds by breathing out, furiously expelling the air—this is the cry.

And then, quite often, everything stops.

As if stunned by such pain, the baby pauses.

Sometimes it cries two or three times before pausing.

And the pause terrifies us. So...we slap the infant, smack the infant, spank the infant.

But now, better trained to control the impulses, trusting in nature and in the steady, continuing pulse of the umbilical cord, we refrain from interfering. And the baby's breathing begins again...by itself. Hesitantly, cautiously at first—still pausing now and again. The baby, still receiving oxygen from the umbilicus, is able to take its time discovering just how much of the burning it can tolerate.

A pause, then another breath. The baby is getting used to this sensation and gradually begins to breathe deeply. Soon it is taking pleasure in what a few moments ago was pain.

In a little while, this breathing is full and abundant, easy and joyous.

The child will have uttered no more than one cry. Or two. Or three. And we will have heard no more than some strenuous gasps—powerful, startled, punctuated by tiny cries—exclamations of surprise and an outburst of energy.

Besides the breathing, we hear other noises: noises the baby makes with its lips, nose, throat.

Lots of noises. A whole language. But no howls of terror, no cries of despair, of agony, of hysteria.

When a child comes into the world, must there be a cry?

Yes, there is no question about it.

But there is no need for weeping.

___

14

Enjoying this new experience, the baby easily loses all memory of the world it just left.

Our baby's birth is an awakening from a happy sleep.

Why should a baby cling to the past when it is so content in this new present?

So. When the umbilicus has finally stopped beating we cut it.

Actually, we cut nothing. It is a dead link that is ready to fall away of itself.

The infant has not been torn from its mother; the two have merely separated.

Later—when this infant takes its first step, ventures into the world standing up—the mother will offer her own friendly support.

The child, still shaky in the legs, will clutch its mother's hand...release her, then reach for her, only to let her go again. Until one day, finally steady on its own legs, it will have no further need of her support, will forget the hand that has been held out for so long.

The hand can then be withdrawn; the child has no more use for it. But what if the mother withdrew her hand while the child was still taking that first step? You might think that in this way she was hastening the child's progress, encouraging its instinct for independence. The odds are that she would be accomplishing the opposite: discouraging, not encouraging her baby.

All of this is equally true in relation to the umbilicus. By not immediately cutting the cord, we let the mother accompany her infant's first steps into the world of breathing. She goes on breathing for them both until her child is safely established in its new domain.

Cutting the umbilicus at the first cry, withdrawing the hand at the first step—they are one and the same thing.

15

We must behave with the most enormous respect toward this instant of birth, this fragile moment.

The baby is between two worlds. On a threshold. Hesitating.

Do not hurry. Do not press. Allow this child to enter.

What an extraordinary thing: this little creature, no longer a fetus, not yet a newborn baby.

This little creature is no longer inside his mother, yet she's still breathing for them both.

An elusive, ephemeral moment.

Leave this child. Alone.

Because this child is free—and frightened.

Don't intrude: stay back. Let time pass.

Grant this moment its slowness, and its gravity.

16

The rest is detail.

Once the respiratory system is functioning, everything has succeeded. (Or if it is not, then the failure is irreparable.)

But even now the details are of vital importance.

How should one place this child on the mother's belly? On its side? Flat on its own belly? On its back?

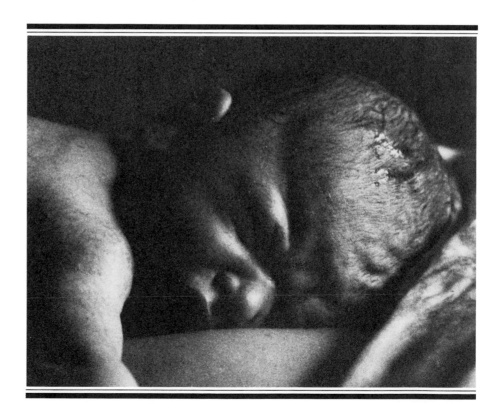

Never on its back. This, in a single spasm, would straighten the spinal column, which has been curved for so long.

The energy that is stored there would be released with such great force, such great violence, that the shock would be unendurable.

Once again, we must remember that it is necessary to let the infant uncoil its spine and stretch its back at its own pace.

Besides, each child is born with its own character, its own temperament.

Some, when they are barely out of their mothers' wombs, straighten out proudly, flex their muscles, stretch their arms.

Their spinal columns straighten out with the force of a tightly strung bow releasing its arrow.

It can also happen that, shaken by their own temerity, they retract and huddle up again.

Others, curled in a ball at first, open themselves more gradually: venture out with great caution.

Since we cannot anticipate what is to come, it is best to place the child on its belly, arms and legs folded under.

This is the age-old, familiar posture, the one that best allows the abdomen to breathe freely and permits the infant to work its way (at its own speed) toward the final unbending.

The stretching, the triumphant extension of self. Moreover, by placing a child on its stomach, we can see its back, watch it in action, observe how it breathes.

In fact, this unbending of the spinal column, this stretching of the back, this start of free respiration are all one.

Watching this breathing, we can see how it pervades the infant's whole body. Not only the thorax but the stomach and—especially —the sides.

Soon the infant appears to be *all* breathing; one sees the powerful waves course through its back from bottom to top, from top to bottom, from the tip of the head to the coccyx.

And then—cautiously emerging from beneath the stomach—an arm, usually the right arm.

The arm stretches out. A hand lightly touches, caresses the mother's stomach—then withdraws.

The other hand ventures out...slowly, as if astonished to encounter no resistance, surprised that the space around it is so vast...

And now the legs begin to move. First one and then the other stretches itself nervously. Then both begin to kick, and thrash—alarmed because there is no longer any barrier to impede them.

To calm their panic, we can offer them support; the touch of a hand, offering gentle resistance even while letting itself be pushed away.

This overcomes the child's horrible sense of having lost its foothold.

And then, suddenly everything is moving together, harmoniously. There is no part of the little body that is not caught up in this movement.

The baby stretches more and more boldly, thrusting, probing.

At this point the child may be placed on its side—its limbs are more relaxed in this position. Its spine adopts the posture that is most comfortable for it.

We move the baby slowly, always lending support, placing one hand under the infant's buttock, and the other high against its back.

It is best not to touch the head at all; the head is extremely sensitive. This was the part of the child that bore the full weight of the birth drama, of the descent into hell; it was this head that cleared the path. Even the slightest touch can now arouse memories that are still too raw.

Finally, when we are sure that everything is functioning well, we place the infant on its back.

Not permanently—the baby is still not comfortable in this new straightening of the spine—but simply as a stage of adjustment.

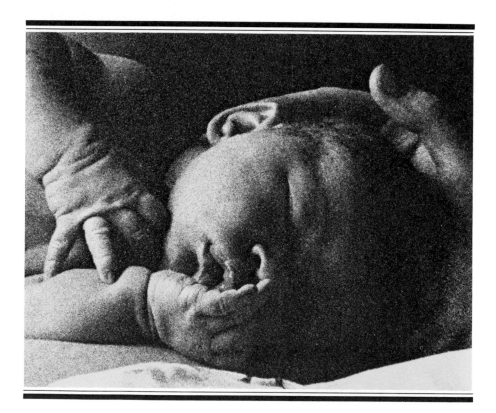

The child is now prepared.

The umbilicus has since been cut when it ceased to beat.

And we are ready for the next step—to raise this baby upright.

Is this not the posture Man has striven for? But even now certain precautions are necessary. We must ease the child *slowly* into a sitting position, always supporting the wavering head. The child's own muscles are not yet strong enough to hold it erect without our help.

17

A word about the hands holding the child.

It is through our hands that we speak to the child, that we communicate.

Touching is the primary language.

"Understanding" comes long after "feeling."

Among blind people, this touching has never lost its subtlety and importance.

Immediately, we sense how important such contact is, just how important is the way we hold a child.

It is a language of skin-to-skin—the skin from which emerge all our sensory organs. And these organs in turn are like window-openings in the wall of skin that both contains and holds us separate from the world.

The newborn baby's skin has an intelligence, a sensitivity that we can only begin to imagine.

It is through this skin that the unborn child once knew its entire world: that is, its mother. It was through the entire surface of its back that it knew her uterus: our backs are, literally, our past.

Now the baby is born. And suddenly this contact is gone. Forever.

Hands touch him. Hands so unlike the uterus in temperature, in weight, in the way they move, in their power, and in their rhythm.

This is the baby's first contact with the unknown, with the new world, with that which is "other."

And our hands that touch and hold the baby, these unknowing, unfeeling hands, have no understanding at all of everything the baby has experienced until this moment.

Our hands are instruments of our intelligence, our will.

They are obedient to the muscles. Voluntary, agile muscles. Their movements are quick, brief, almost brusque.

And terrifying to the infant who has experienced only the slow internal rhythms of the womb.

How could the child *not* panic at this new kind of touch? And how, then, ought we to touch—to handle—a newborn baby?

Very simply: by remembering what this infant has just left behind. By never forgetting that everything new and unknown might terrify and that everything recognizable and familiar is reassurance.

To calm the infant in this strange, incomprehensible world into which it just emerged, it is necessary—and enough—that the hands holding him should speak in the language of the womb.

What does this mean?

That the hands must "remember" the slowness, the continuous movement of the uterine contraction, the "peristaltic wave" the child grew to know so well during the final months before its birth.

This is another reason why it is necessary to first place the child flat on its stomach—so that, in massaging it, we "speak" to its back.

And what should our hands say? Exactly what the mother and her womb have been saying.

Not the womb as it was during final labor, not the violent womb that expels and banishes. But the womb of the early, happy days.

The womb that pressed slowly, tenderly. The womb that embraced. The womb that was pure love.

It was an infinitely sensual, amorous relationship that existed between the child and its mother, between the uterus and its prisoner.

What is needed is neither a brisk rubbing motion nor a caress, but a deep and slow massage.

Our hands travel over the infant's back, one after the other, following each other like waves. One hand still in contact as the other begins. Each maintaining its steady rhythm until its entire journey is concluded. Without rediscovering this visceral slowness that lovers rediscover instinctively, it is impossible to communicate with the child.

But, people will say, you're making love to the child!

Yes, almost.

To make love is to return to paradise, it is to plunge again into the world before birth, before the great separation. It is to find again the primordial slowness, the blind and all-powerful rhythm of the internal world, of the great ocean. Making love is the great regression.

What we are doing here is softening the pain of an almost total upheaval by carrying the past forward into the present. We are giving the child company on its journey. We are soothing by sending the echo of the familiar and loving uterine waves along its back.

Yes, making love is the sovereign remedy for anguish: to make

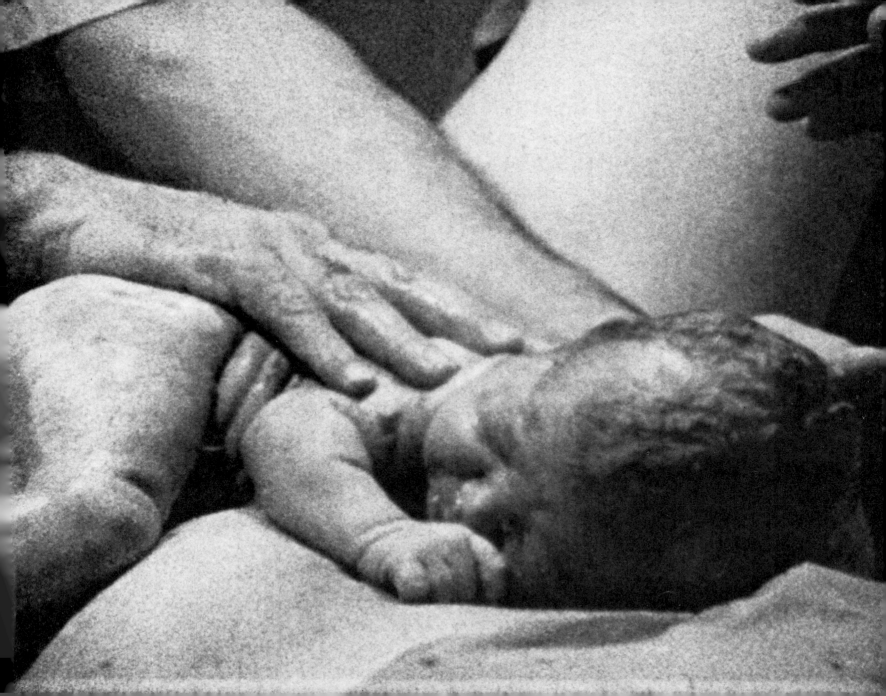

love is to rediscover peace and harmony. In the cataclysm of birth is it not fit that we should call upon this sovereign comfort?

18

But our hands may also remain immobile.

The hands that touch the child reveal everything to it: nervousness or calm, clumsiness or confidence, tenderness or violence.

The child knows if the hands are loving. Or if they are careless. Or worse, if they are rejecting.

In attentive and loving hands, a child abandons itself, opens itself up.

In rigid and hostile hands, a child retreats into itself, blocks out the world.

So that before we even think of recreating the prenatal rhythms which once flowed around this little body, we must let our hands lie on it motionless.

Not hands that are inert, perfunctory, distracted.

But hands that are attentive, alive, alert, responsive to its slightest quiver.

Hands that are light. That neither command nor demand. That are simply there.

Light...and heavy in the weight of tenderness. And of silence.

19

Whose hands should hold the child? The mother's, naturally, provided that these hands know...everything we have been saying.

But that cannot be taught. Although it can be forgotten.

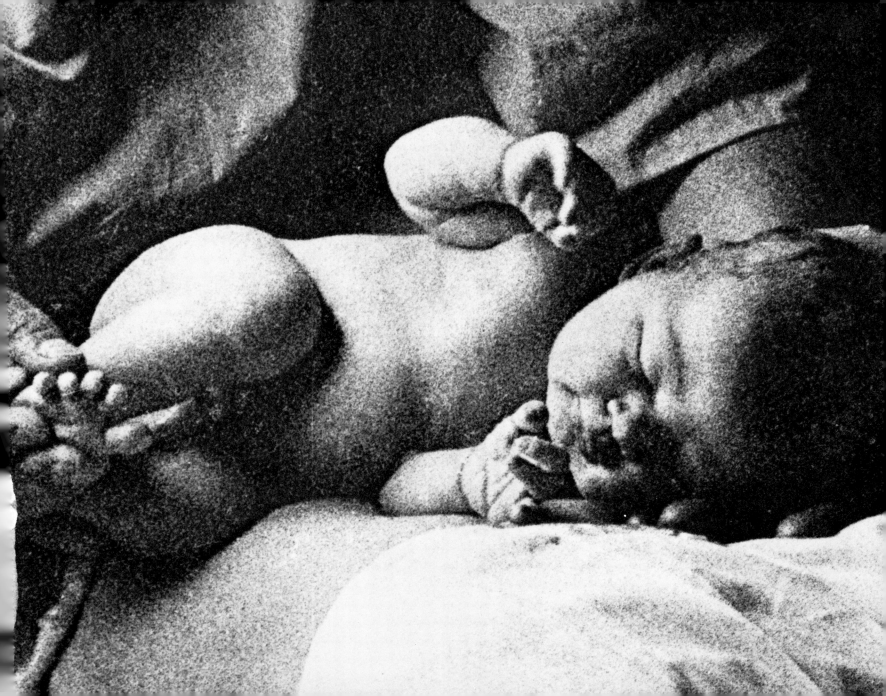

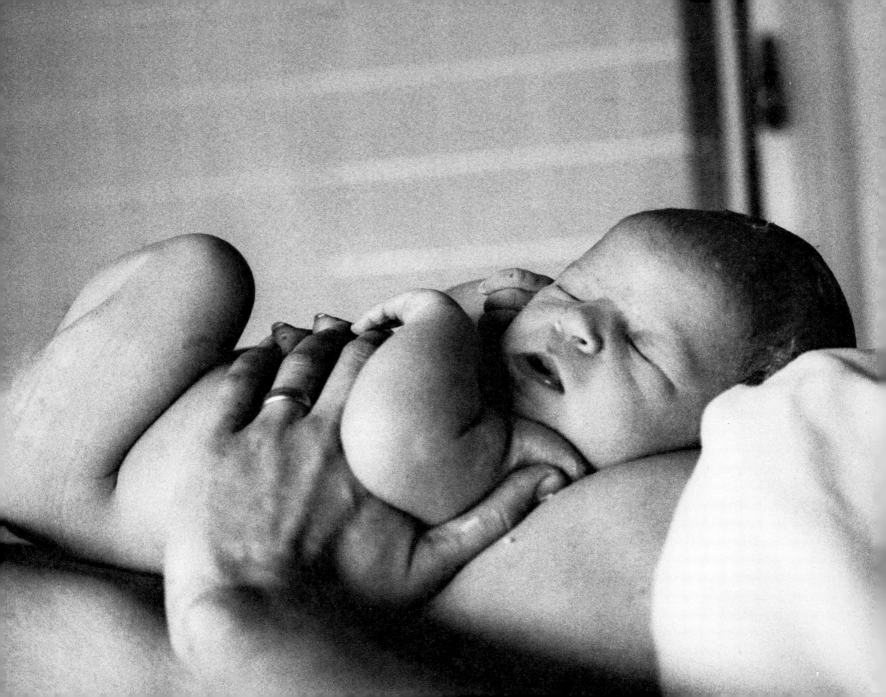

How many mothers briskly pat their babies! Or shake them, while believing that they're rocking and caressing them…

How many have hands that are stiff, lifeless, lacking understanding!

How many preoccupied by their own emotions actually threaten to smother their children!

Happily, in most cases the woman who has delivered her baby naturally knows her own body. She is ready to hold and touch her baby. She has had to rediscover her own body, to control its negative impulses.

Such a woman, despite the joy which fills her, will not overwhelm her child.

When the newborn child is placed on her stomach, when she lays her hands on it, she will remember, "My trial is over. But not my baby's."

Yes, the delivery is over but the baby's awakening has just begun. The baby is on the first step of a glorious adventure—and yet is transfixed with fear.

Do not move. Do not add to the baby's panic.

Just be there. Without moving. Without getting impatient. Without asking anything.

At this point, out of consideration for her child, out of real—not egocentric—love, a woman will simply place her hands on its body. And leave them there, immobile.

Hands that are not animated, agitated, trembling with emotion, but are calm and light. Hands of peace.

Through such hands flow the waves of love which will assuage her baby's anguish.

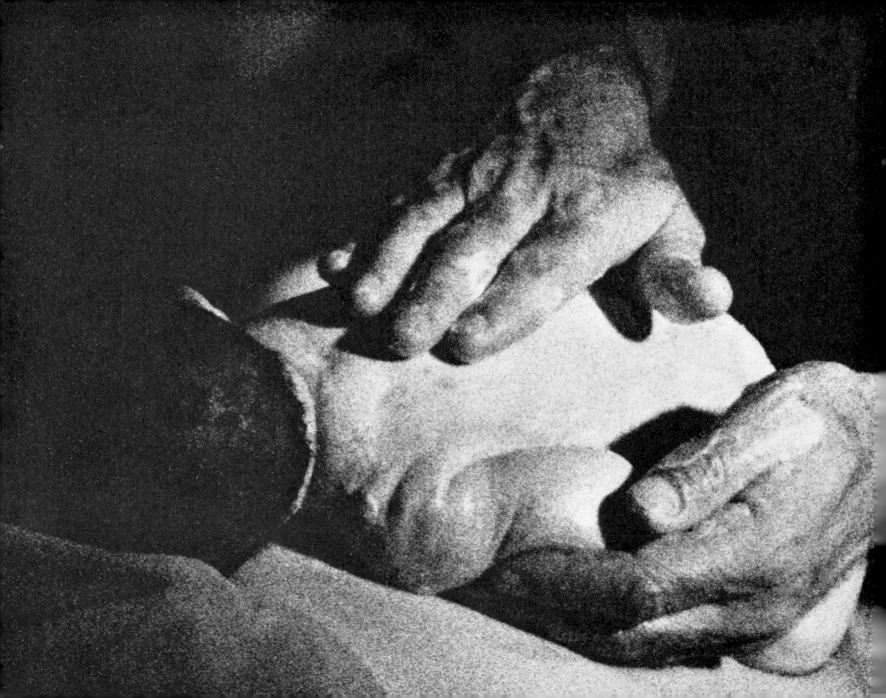

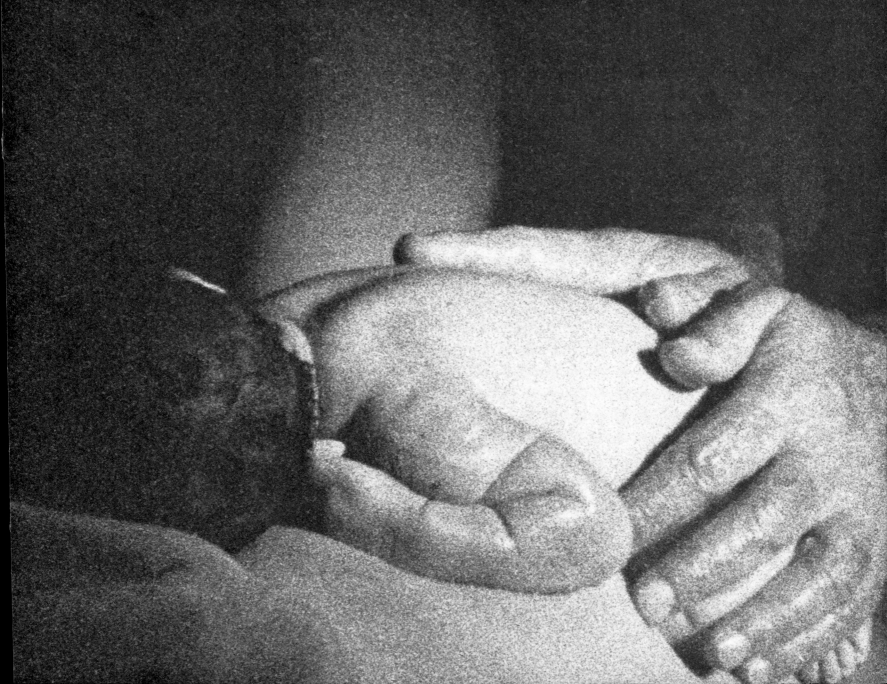

20

Anguish?

Yes, anguish. Yet one more thing to surprise us! It is easy to accept that a child can feel fear and pain. But anguish?

Nonetheless, it is so.

The idea people generally have of birth is that the child takes no personal part in it. That the child is passive, merely submitting to expulsion.

That it is the mother who does all the work.

But the reality is totally different.

The Greeks, as we know from Hippocrates, believed that it was the child who demanded to be born.

They believed that when pregnancy reached its term, the child was beginning to lack for food. Feeling its life threatened, it was forced to abandon the dark cavern which had been its home until then, to search for the way out—using its feet to propel itself forward, to force its way toward freedom.

We have laughed at these old wives' tales, only to discover...that all this is perfectly true!

We have discovered today that the stimulus that sets labor in motion comes from the child, just as the Ancients said it did. And now we know that the child actually does struggle to be born.

The acceleration of its heartbeat indicates both the enormous effort it is making and the terror it feels. And an alert mother, conscious of what is happening within her body, recognizes the exact moment when both she and her child are both beginning their desperate exertions.

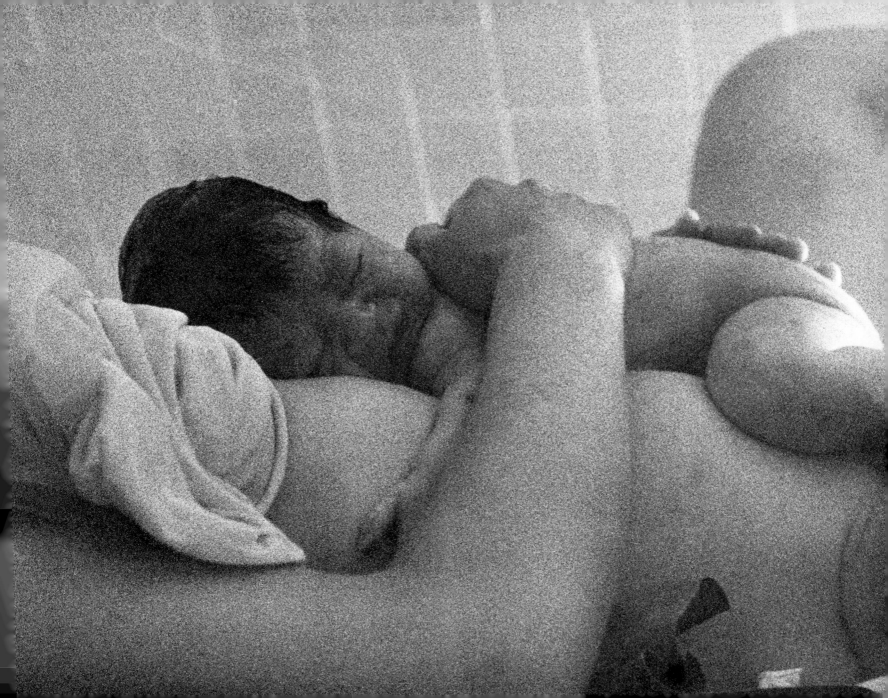

Her child struggles. Fiercely. For its life. And it is a fight to the death. It is "the mother" or "the child."

And when this child does emerge—when the battle is won—his mother is suddenly gone.

And what the child feels is intolerable anguish: "I am alive, but I have killed my mother. I am here, but my mother is gone!"

This seems incredible to us. And yet it is so. Those who have relived their birth can testify to it.

Here too, it is necessary to reassure, to pacify the child immediately.

Through her hands that do not move, yet that are charged with tenderness, the mother is saying to her baby:

"Don't be afraid; I'm here. We're both safe, you and I; we're both alive."

21

How important this first contact is, this first meeting of mother and child!

Many mothers do not know how to touch their babies. Or, to be more exact, do not dare. They are paralyzed.

Many will not admit it. Or are not even conscious of it.

But it is true nevertheless, if you can recognize the signs.

There is something that restrains these mothers. Some profound inhibition.

This new body has emerged from what modesty has led us to call, by a curious euphemism, the "private parts."

Whatever circumlocution we use, our education has still condi-

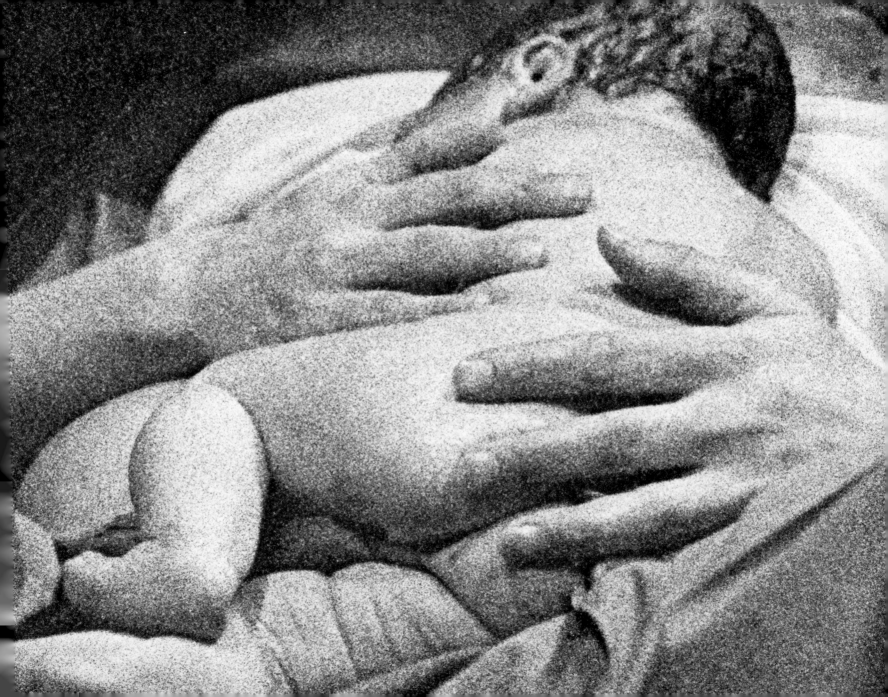

tioned most of us to consider these parts of the body as dirty. To reject them. Not to mention them.

But the baby has come from there.

From this region of the body that we are meant to know nothing about, that we don't examine, that we don't display or touch. That we would deny.

Now this something has emerged from "there." Something warm and sticky. And the result of muscular efforts that resemble those we use in excreting.

And it is this "something" that we must touch!

The old prohibition holds sway: Don't touch! Not nice!

Touch "this"? Impossible.

Moreover, how can we place our hands on that which has just come from inside a human stomach? Human entrails?

The mother remains paralyzed.

Seized by a profound confusion, she no longer knows *what* she feels for this "thing" that is there, on her belly. An immense disgust? A passionate interest?

Sometimes it is necessary to gently take her hands and place them on the child.

Her resistance is obvious. But once it is overcome, once the step has been taken, what she (and we) feel is extraordinary.

She has just transcended what is taboo.

The barrier has fallen that separated her from her child. And from herself.

She is filled with an indescribable joy.

The old distinction between good and bad, clean and dirty, permissible and forbidden, has dissolved.

Suddenly, things are so simple. They are what they are, and

nothing more. For the first time in a lifetime!

No more traces of fear.

By touching her child, the woman has at last discovered herself. Has made herself whole.

For her, the internal and the external have fused.

22

And now let us look again at the child, who by this time is breathing normally.

The umbilicus has been severed, all that is now far in the past...

Just how far? It could be years. But measured by a watch, it is perhaps three minutes; six at the most. And yet our concentration has been so intense that we have been existing outside time.

And where exactly are we? This calm, this silence, contrast so dramatically with the howls that accompany so many births...

Just as the mother's tranquillity during natural childbirth still has the power to amaze—almost to unnerve—us, the peace and serenity of the baby she bears takes us by surprise.

Yet miraculous as this calm and silence are, a still greater miracle awaits us.

The child is about to leave the mother once more.

The two have touched, have rediscovered each other. Now they are going to separate.

A new step for the child on the road to freedom.

But we must take great care over this new separation.

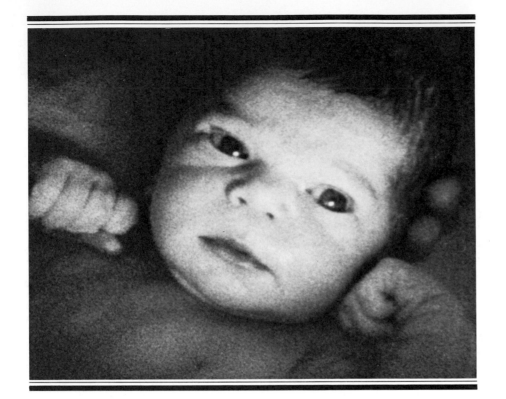

Where do we place the child? What must we do to ensure that this separation is not a shock, but a joy?

How do we banish, once and for all, the fear that is still so close to the surface? How do we loosen all the knots of tension that may escape our eye but are revealed to the touch when we place our hands on the baby's back?

It is easy. The child is abandoning the warmth and softness of its mother's belly. We can ensure that it finds a similar warmth and softness elsewhere.

Let's not place a newborn infant on a metal scale, with all its hard coldness. Nor in fabrics that feel rough after the mother's smoothness and warmth.

Let us place the infant, replace it rather, into water!

For the baby has emerged from water, the maternal waters that have carried it, caressed and cradled it. Made it light as a bird…

A bath has been prepared in a basin. At the temperature of the body or thereabouts—ninety-eight or ninety-nine degrees.

We place the child in it.

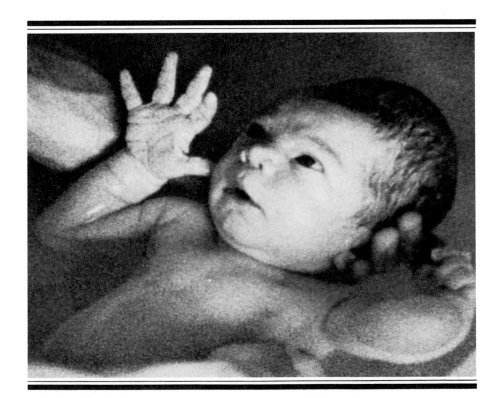

Once again, extremely slowly.

As the baby sinks down, it becomes weightless, and is set free of the body that is overwhelming it—this body with all its burden of harsh new sensation.

The infant floats. Disembodied. Light. As free as in the early, distant days of pregnancy, when it could play, could move about without restrictions in a limitless sea.

Its surprise, its joy are boundless.

In its element once more, the infant forgets what it has just left behind; forgets its mother. It has returned inside her!

This first separation, far from being an agony, becomes a joy.

The hands supporting the child in the bath soon feel the little body relax in complete abandon. Everything that was fear, stiffness, tension, now melts like snow in the sun. Everything in the infant's body that was still anxious, frozen, blocked, begins to live, to dance.

And—a miracle—the child opens its eyes wide.

This first look is unforgettable.

Immense, deep, grave, intense, these eyes say: "Where am I? What has happened to me?"

We feel in this baby such utter concentration, such astonishment, such depth of curiosity, that we are overcome.

We discover that beyond any doubt, a *person* is there. Who had been hidden behind fear. Whose eyes had been held shut by terror.

We see—what should have been obvious—that far from being a beginning, birth is only a passage. And that this creature who is looking at us, questioning us, "has been" already for a long time.

Everyone who has been present at these births, who has seen these infants open their eyes, who has felt the weight of their

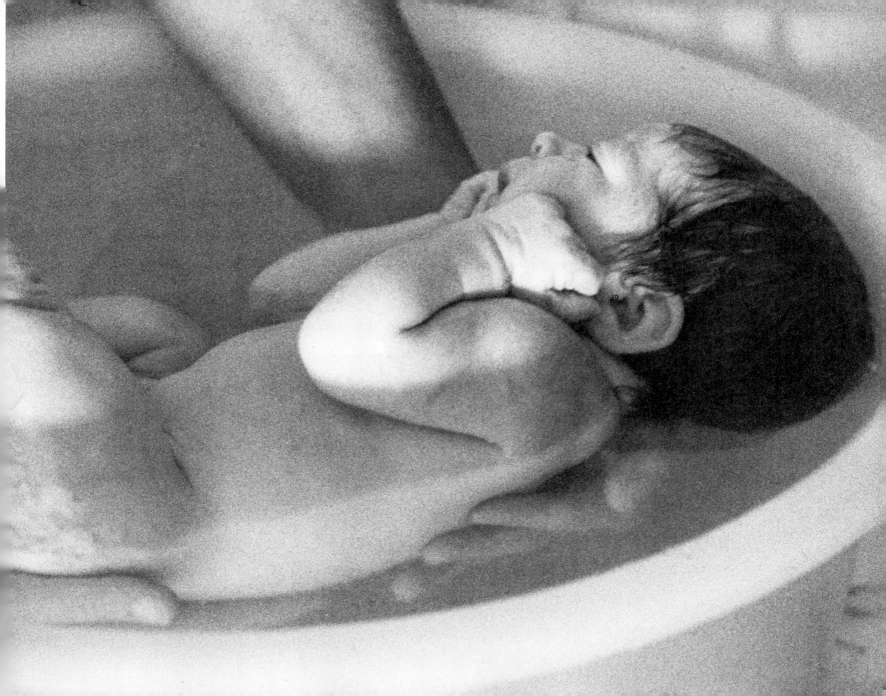

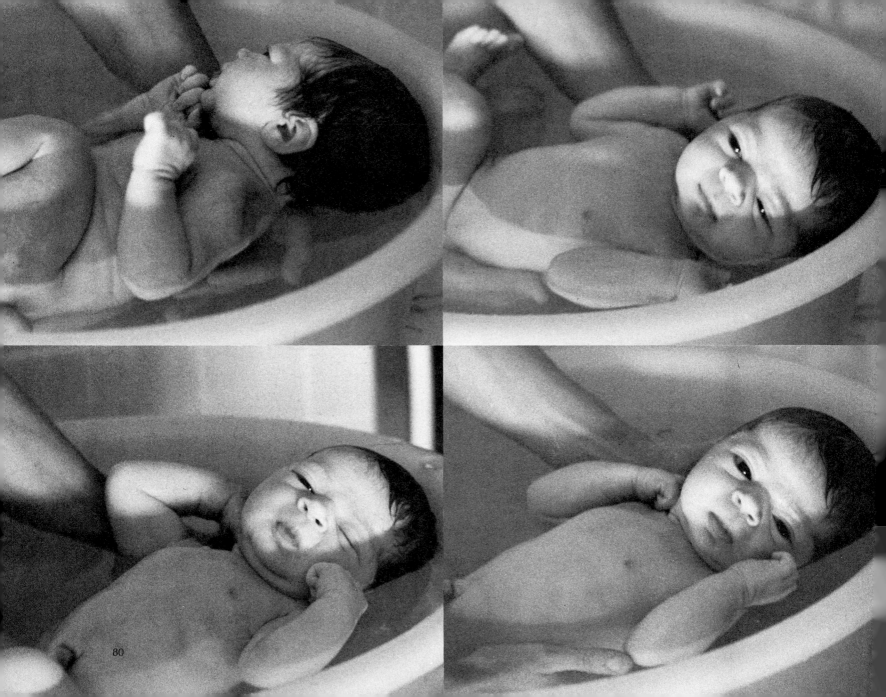

80

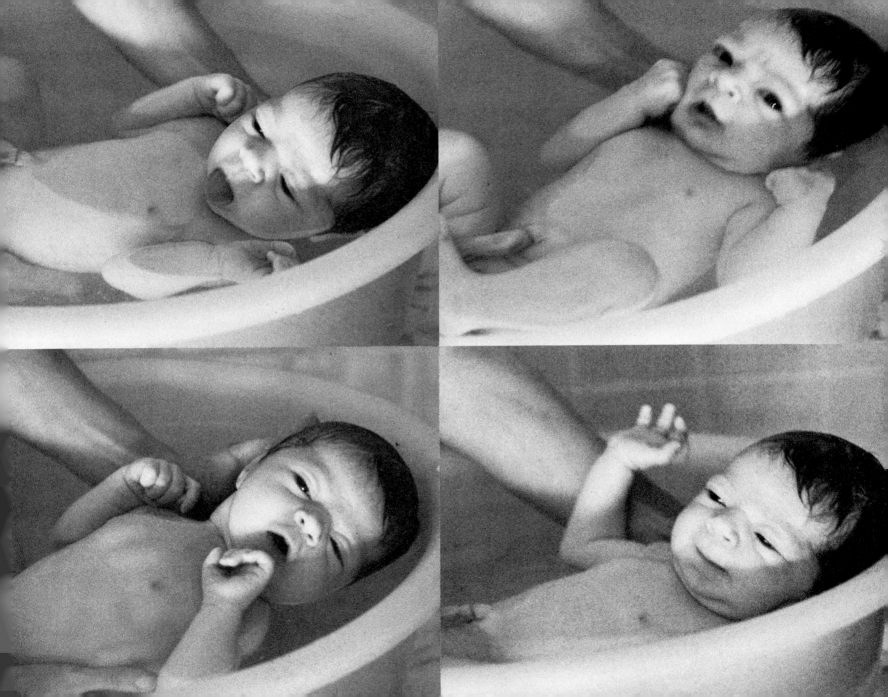

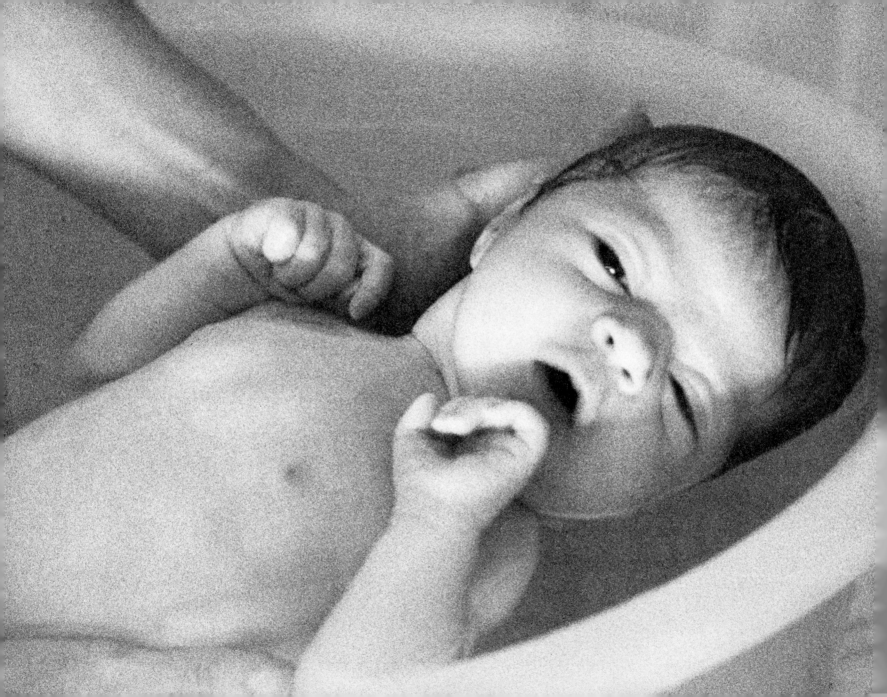

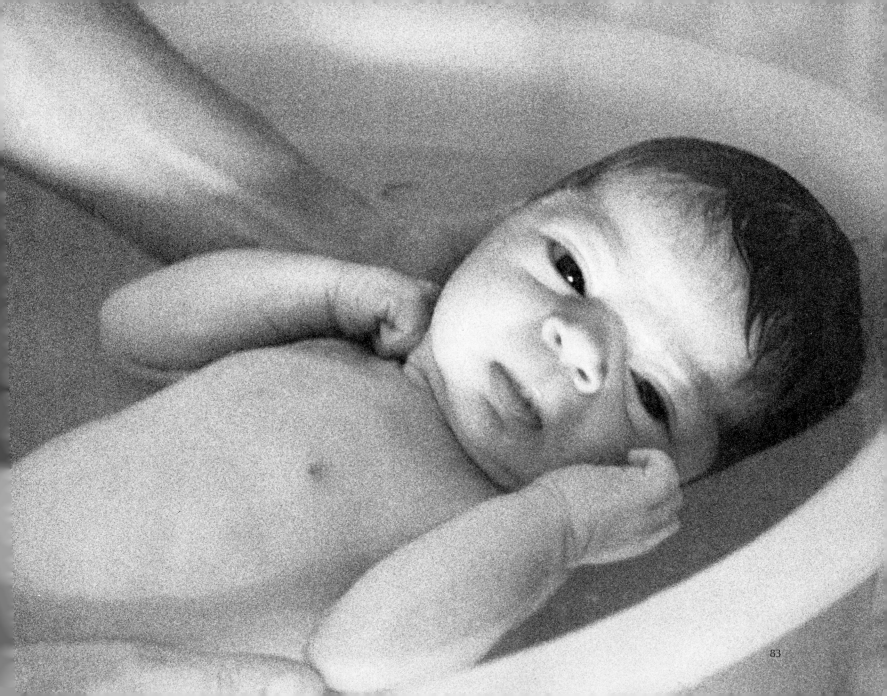

curiosity—everyone has cried out with the same incredulity: "But...it's not possible...the baby can see!"

Do babies "see" in our sense of the word? Undoubtedly not; they don't receive images as we receive them.

But that they communicate in their own way, in a way that we have almost totally lost, is something which can no longer be doubted.

"A newborn baby is blind, it doesn't hear anything, feel anything. It's not yet conscious. How could you imagine that at this age..."

Before the questioning intensity of those eyes, such assumptions make us smile. And fill us with shame.

23

And what happens next is no less amazing.

Having moved from immediate fear and shock at its new condition to an enchanted acceptance of it, the child now begins to explore this kingdom which is to be its home.

Movement, now, is everything.

The head turns—to the right, to the left—slowly, twisting around as far as the neck will allow.

The face is in perfect profile.

A hand stirs—opens, closes—and emerges from the water. The arm follows, rising. The hand caresses the sky, feels the space around it, falls again.

The other hand rises in its turn, traces an arabesque, and then, in its turn, descends.

Now they play together, meet, embrace, separate.

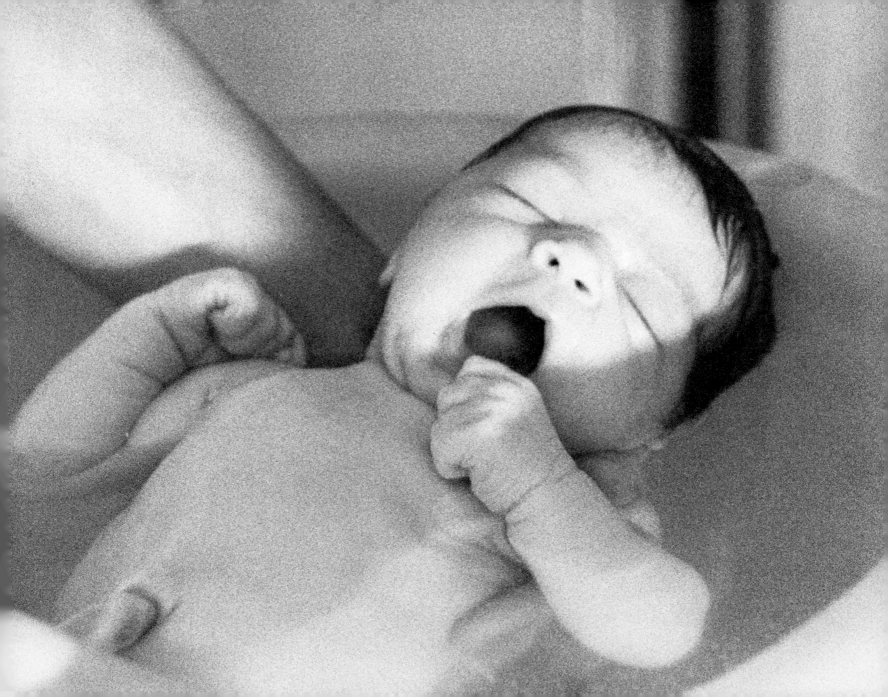

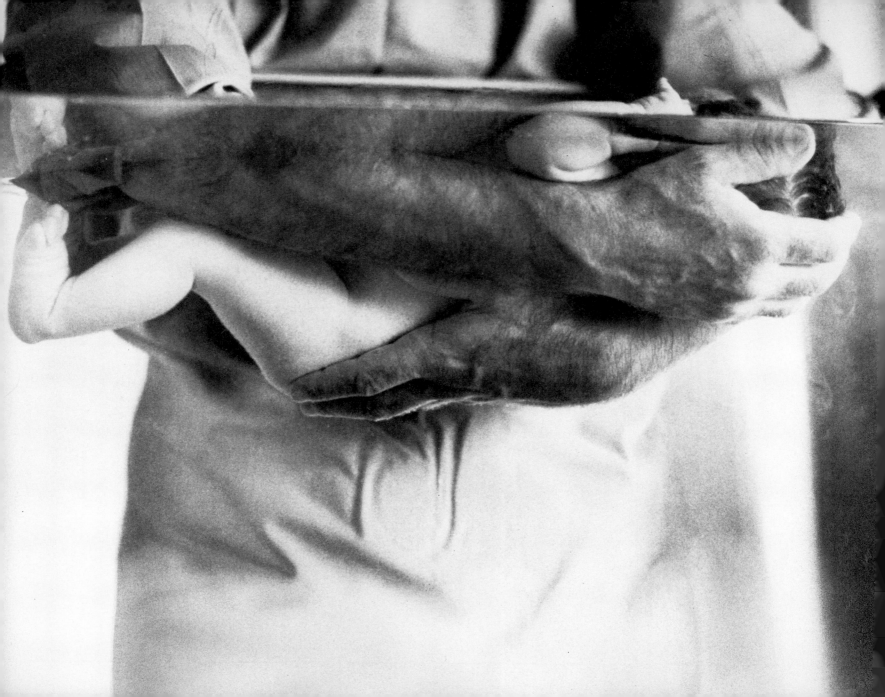

One moves away, the other darts after it.

One pauses, dreams, opens and closes with the slowness of the sea. The other falls under the same spell. The two dreams mirror each other: hands like flowers about to blossom. Sea anemones, they breathe with the slow cradling rhythm of the world beneath the ocean, moved by its invisible currents.

The legs—at first timid in motion, not daring to enter into the game—begin moving too. Abruptly, a foot shoots out. And then the other, hitting the edge of the tub, propelling the whole body of the

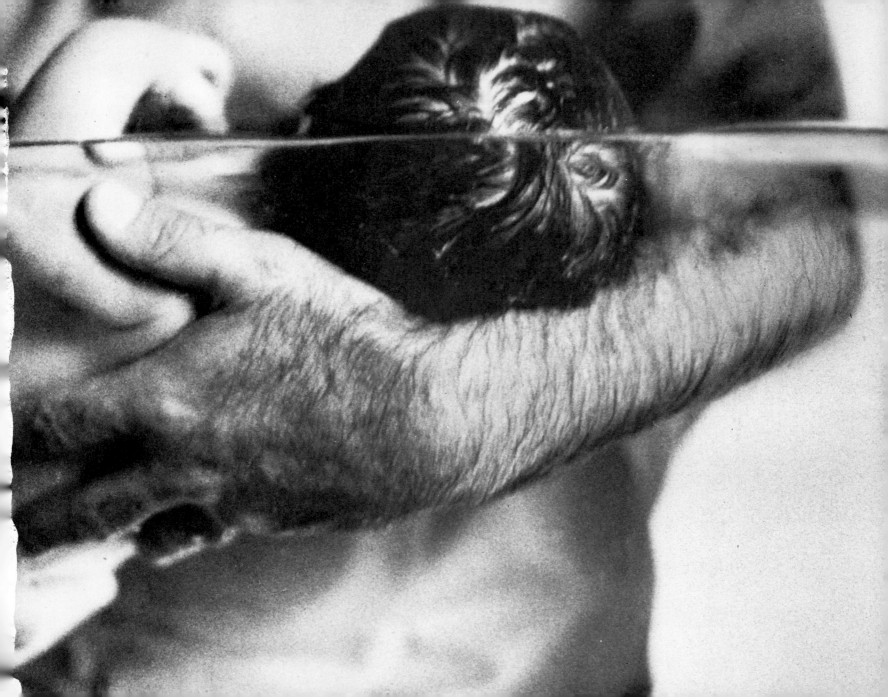

infant backward. The child is reveling in its adventure.

And then it happens again.

The child is playing!

And not ten minutes have gone by since it was born!

This entire ballet is taking place in profound silence, punctuated only by soft little cries—exclamations of surprise and joy.

Sometimes solemn, sometimes playful, completely absorbed in its discoveries, the child explores, tests the space inside, outside, around it with a concentration that never falters, that never succumbs to distractions.

Totally *there*, an impassioned observer of its own body.

A happy, a *blissful* child, it is a unity, a continuity, a totality. Not an inch of its body is alien to its movements. Every inch of this child is moving, moving together, living in a most complete harmony.

Must we not envy this baby, we who are so fragmented, who have lost this primal unity? We who always are—or would be—elsewhere? We who are incapable of being, simply, "there"?

And now the face begins to come alive. The mouth opens, closes. The lips part. The tongue flicks out, retreats. And when finally, as if by accident, a hand encounters the face, slides over it, finds the mouth, the child pushes a thumb into it and sucks.

The hand moves on. Travels once more through space, and returns to this paradise, the mouth.

And this time the child would like to get its whole hand inside...

Yes, this new world is an enchanted place. How could the child possibly regret the past?

Doubtless there are enemies lurking in the new world; hunger has not yet reared its ugly head.

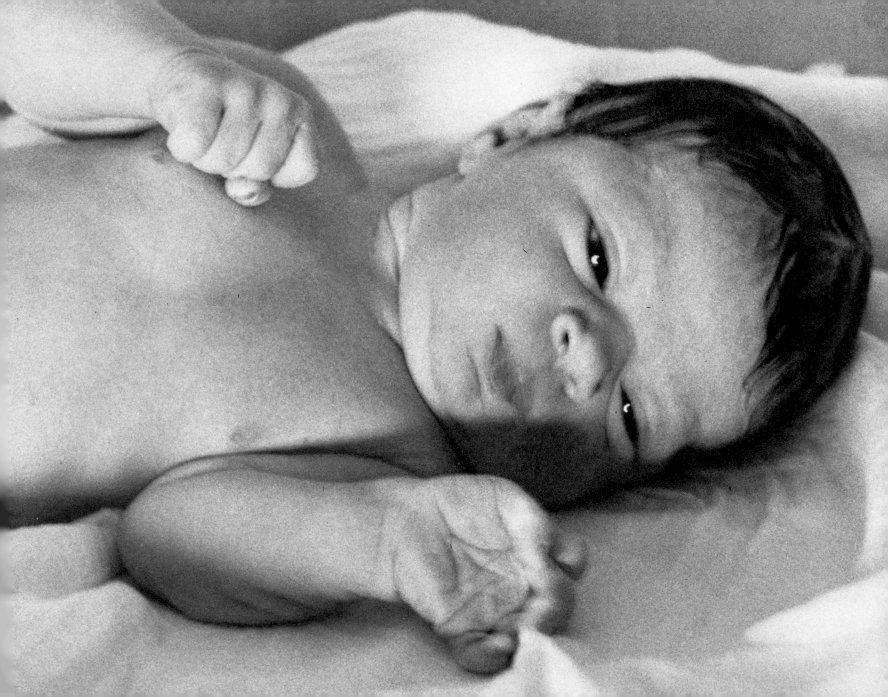

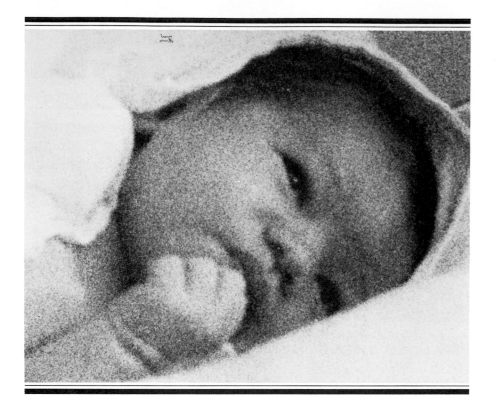

It doesn't matter. Everything has begun so well that the child will enjoy forever a taste for adventure.

How long should we leave the child in its bath? It is for the child to decide.

We should be sure the relaxation is complete, that there isn't the least resistance in the little body, the least hesitation, the smallest tension, the slightest stiffness, the merest knot, the shadow of a doubt.

We should be sure that everything is in motion. That everything is joy.

24

Now that all fear has been dispelled, now that birth and all that came before it are forgotten, it is time to emerge at last from the comforting waters. Time for the baby to take its place on terra firma.

The fourth step in the path of birth. The fourth stage.

The infant is going to be born yet again into its new element. Of its own accord.

Leaving the water, the baby finds another new master, another tyrant: the weight of gravity; the new burden of its own body.

If a baby is not to be overcome by this, if it is to accept these new bonds readily, things must once again become a game. The baby must enjoy itself. So we lift it slowly from the water—as slowly as formerly we immersed it. It rediscovers its body's weight—and cries out. We plunge it back in. Its body is gone again! We take it out once more.

A powerful sensation, and one that is now no longer new, it has become as pleasurable as it is now familiar. So powerful and so pleasurable that every child ever born longs to experience it again.

At home with itself now, enjoying the world it is to live in, the baby is now ready to end its bath.

We place it on a diaper that has been made warm for it.

We wrap it in layers of cotton and wool—the world is a cold place. We cover neither the head nor the hands, which must be free to move and play.

We place the baby on its side—*not,* of course, on its back.

Its arms and legs can move at its ease; its abdomen can expand and contract as it breathes; its head can turn freely.

We have taken care to support the baby's back, to steady it, so that the back senses "something" there, and is reassured.

And then we leave the baby to itself.

The fifth step, the fifth stage on the path of birth.

For the first time the child is alone. And discovers...immobility. An extraordinary experience.

And terrifying, once again, in its utter strangeness.

For nine months, the baby has been an eternal voyager. Its shifting world has never ceased to move. Sometimes gently, sometimes violently. Wasn't its mother's body always in motion? And even when she was still or asleep, there was always the great rhythm of her breathing, of her diaphragm.

The baby has lived in perpetual motion.

Now, a truly appalling change: everything stops.

For the first time.

Nothing moves.

The world has frozen, died.

It is the unknown.

A baby helped into the world the conventional way is seized by panic at this point, begins to howl in its terror and bewilderment.

Later on, every time it is reminded of this sudden sense of total immobility, of this solitude, the same panic will seize it again, and it will start to howl once more, its anguish stemming not so much from being left alone as from believing that the world is once again dead. Frozen in the ice of immobility.

Then someone will cradle the baby, and it will reencounter the beloved yet terrifying storm of motion, and will be appeased. It will relive the first moment of its life, proceeding from agony to agony every time that it is picked up, held, put down again, and left alone.

But our adventurer is free of fear. He or she has gone from change to change, from one discovery to the next, so slowly, so surrounded and enveloped in love and attention, that everything

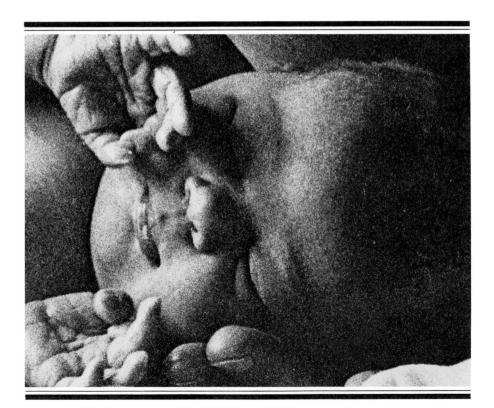

that happens is accepted with confidence and happiness. Nothing startles.

At the very moment when other newborn babies are beginning to howl and sob more violently than ever, our baby remains silent.

At this moment of transformation, our baby can close its eyes and utter a single cry.

A cry of surprise.

Never sobs of distress and pain. Never panic, never fear.

At most, a cry of anger—the baby objecting to the end of its pleasure.

Protesting against the bath being over. Expressing itself.

But discovering another, greater pleasure; experiencing something still more extraordinary. Our baby reopens its eyes. Grows quiet. And—in silent astonishment—tastes the unknown: stillness.

The world of perpetual motion has become the world of constant stability. The storm has permanently abated; the child has reached serenity.

At present, it is utterly lost in the joy of discovery. Movement has not ceased; it is no longer outside, but within.

Inside the child, everything is moving. Harmoniously.

The eyes remain wide open, passionately involved. The arms, the legs continue their ballet. The hands endlessly explore.

The mask of fear has disappeared forever.

Yes, now we are on firm ground. Our odyssey has ended.

The other monsters which await us may materialize—hunger; all the thousand natural shocks that flesh is heir to. We will know how to meet them.

The quiet, newborn baby radiates the most intense peace.

Completely awake, supremely alert, this baby glows.

Yes, it is the child-king, a holy infant. The one of whom the Scriptures say: "Except ye be as little children..."

And Lao-tse: "The one whose abounding grace overflows, the perfect one, here like the newborn child."

What is this "abounding grace" that emanates from the saints? And from newborn babies?

We are touching on mysteries now.

This is a grace which radiates in silence that crowns with a halo every child who arrives among us.

PART THREE

In the pursuit of learning, every day something is acquired.
In the pursuit of Tao, every day something is dropped.

Less and less is done.
Until nonaction is achieved.
When nothing is done, nothing is left undone.

The world is ruled by letting things take their course.
It cannot be ruled by interfering.

— Tao Te Ching

And we, also, are at the end of a great adventure. We are about to leave this baby, to return it for a while to its mother, now that it has savored the joys of solitude and stillness.

Lying once again on the beloved body of the mother, its ear against her heart, the baby rediscovers the familiar steady beat.

All is accomplished. All is perfect.

These two who have battled so fiercely are at one with each other again.

And we too are fully content: we have understood.

We wished to know why it was that birth was so appalling.

We said: "If only we could understand why these poor newborn babies cry out..."

Understand what these infants are telling us with their flailing arms and legs, with their heads, their hands, their backs—with their screams.

They are telling us: "I am in pain, I am suffering."

And even more desperately: "I am in terror."

The fear and the pain are one.

They are trying to express exactly what their mothers have expressed—also without words.

Who is natural enough, who is unselfconscious enough, to dare say: "I am afraid"?

Women *didn't* dare.

But their bodies proclaimed it! The bodies of women in labor were nothing more than a mass of spasms, tensions, frantic heavings, locked muscles. Their bodies wanting only to escape, to deny what was taking place—mute testimony to their crazed panic and terror.

Exorcising this fear has freed women from the agony of childbirth, so that now, at times, it can become almost an ecstasy.

By sparing the child this severe terror, we can transform its birth into a comparably rich delight.

2

To protect newborn children from fear, we must unveil the world to them infinitely slowly, in an endless sequence of severely limited revelations. And not overwhelm them with more new sensations than they can support and integrate.

In doing this, it is essential to reinforce memories and impressions of the past; to forge a link between past and present; to ensure that in this totally unknown and seemingly antagonistic universe, some familiar thing is there to reassure and appease.

Once more let us try to imagine what it is that makes this rite of passage so appalling.

Our adult senses have lost that first acuteness, that first total sensitivity. But, more important, they have been compartmentalized.

Each sense is occupied only with itself.

Sophisticated systems filter and organize our sense impressions into coherent perceptions, give them logic and meaning. And this conditioning is so ingrained in us that we are no longer conscious of it.

Our conditioning, our *language*, hide variety from us. Protect us from its overpowering totality.

But this in no way is the case with the newborn infant.

Sensation is total: not filtered, not organized.

An awkward movement, a moment of inattention, of overeagerness, and all is lost.

The child begins to cry.

3

We also have asked: "What is the mystery, the 'thing,' that keeps us from seeing this new being in its separate reality?"

We know now that this "thing" is ourselves. It is "I," the ego, our conditioning. What we are.

Our custom of cutting the umbilicus only moments after the infant has been born is a remarkable instance of our blindness.

"How is it," we ask ourselves, "that Man, a rational animal of reputed intelligence, acts so irrationally at so important a moment?"

Why do we do it?

Anyone present at a birth has got to be profoundly unsettled—whether obstetrician or attendant, whether having witnessed ten births or ten thousand.

No doubt this is because we have all experienced birth. And the experience echoes deep inside us, as potent as it is suppressed.

Nothing is forgotten—birth least of all. Only its immediate imprint has been blurred.

Thus the doctor and his associates find themselves profoundly but unconsciously involved in every birth they participate in.

And there is a change in our breathing in moments of greatest emotional tension—this, also, unconsciously.

As the climax of every delivery approaches, emotions intensify.

Do we realize how contagious this is, and how it feeds upon itself?

When the infant makes its first appearance, emotion is at its height. And everyone's breathing—already tight—chokes, stops altogether.

"Will the baby breathe?"

We are holding our own breath. Identifying with the baby, however unconsciously.

We have all *returned* to our own births—fighting for breath just like this newborn baby; close to suffocation.

And *we* don't have the umbilicus to supply us with oxygen. So things quickly become unbearable.

It's necessary to "*do* something."

The easiest, the most sensible, the most obvious thing for the onlooker to do—would be simply to breathe.

Instead of which, he cuts the baby's umbilicus.

His own emotional involvement has made him irrational.

Naturally, the infant howls.

Each person present exclaims in relief: "He's breathing!"

Poor fool! It's only himself he has relieved.

What he really should be crying out is: "*I* am breathing!"

Because the truth is that the baby was in no hurry—its umbilicus was allowing it plenty of time.

Under the pretext of aiding this new and "other" being, the attendant has considered only himself.

Without knowing it, he has made a transference. He has rid himself of his own anguish by projecting it onto the child.

And it is this sacrificial lamb, deprived of his umbilicus, who suddenly is choking.

And howling...

To relieve *our* breathing.

This process of transference will be endlessly repeated. And the sum of these repetitions is what we, in our ignorance, call education.

4

What remains unsaid?

At the risk of being tedious, we must return yet again to the baby's cry—the cry that was our point of departure.

"Must the infant cry?"

This question is of paramount importance. Too much is at stake here to risk misunderstandings.

The answer is clear and simple: "Yes, the infant must cry."

And it is essential that the cry be what is called "a good cry." Resonant, vigorous. A clear cry in which the baby's whole body participates.

This cry—this total bodily response—confirms that all is well.

If the child is born "stupefied," if it is listless, if it is wailing instead of crying, every step should be taken *instantly* to produce a clear, satisfactory sound.

This much is obvious—and there should be no possibility of misunderstanding.

In the same way, if the infant coming into the world is being strangled by its umbilicus, we should not hesitate for an instant to cut it and set the baby free.

All this is common sense. Just as one wouldn't train a woman for natural childbirth when it was certain she required a Caesarean.

Perhaps it may seem that in these few lines we have negated everything we have said until now.

Not at all.

It is essential that the child cry when being born.

Once. Or twice.

And that is enough.

Then the child must breathe. Or if it cries, then its cries must be those of strength, of vitality, of gratification.

Not cries of misery, of terror, of desolation.

No wails! No sobs!

You don't need to have a particularly sensitive or trained ear to tell the difference. You only need to be properly attentive to recognize the large and varied range a newborn baby's voice already possesses. And how many things it can tell us...without speaking.

It takes only the slightest concentration to differentiate between the cry of life, the cry of satisfaction, and the cry of sorrow, of pain, the cry of fear.

This being so, can every child awake to life as peaceably as the one we have described?

Is it possible that all of them need utter only a cry or two and then begin to breathe and murmur softly?

Certainly not.

Any more than one can promise every woman that she will come through childbirth without any pain.

In both experiences, everything is possible.

Each person is different. Each is unique, mysterious, unpredictable.

Sometimes a woman who seems to be physically unsuited will astonish us by her powers, while others, apparently better endowed by nature, encounter unforeseen obstacles.

106

In the same way, each child arrives among us with its own temperament and character and heredity, its own destiny.

Each reacts in its own way. And it is a miracle to see how uniquely different each one is.

Two newborn babies don't resemble each other any more than an Eskimo and a Papuan do.

And yet...

Curiously, during the first moments, all newborn babies are alike. For a brief period, it is still as if they had no identity at all.

Identity will come quickly. Soon it will no longer be possible to confuse them. But during those first few moments, they have a disturbing oneness.

It is simply that they all wear the same mask. The depersonalizing mask of terror.

And it is only when this mask falls away that we discover the individual beneath.

Although every child is unique, every child must pass through the same stages leading from an enclosed world to the open one, from being folded in on itself, to reaching outward.

Each baby travels this path in its own manner.

And we should not always assume that those who travel most quickly will fare best.

Some babies seem to bound into life, then suddenly withdraw into their own anger.

Others go on struggling, eyes tight shut, incapable of realizing that their ordeal is over, that they have been born. It is immensely difficult wresting them from their nightmares, from their fears.

Others emerge casually, barely utter a cry, open their eyes, and begin to play!

Still others make their way slowly, calmly, majestically.

It is so very true that each infant arrives with its own temperament.

But in every case, once the child has opened its eyes, the battle is over and won.

We can even say that only at this moment is the child really born.

It has surfaced now, it has truly emerged. And at this same moment, the mask falls away and the individual person appears.

Another surprise: there are no ugly infants.

Yet when the newborn baby arrives, very often it *seems* ugly…and confronted with such a distressing face, we may recoil in instinctive rejection. Certain newborn infants are frightful.

But it is only a mask. The mask of terror. *Always.*

It is almost impossible to imagine to what degree a face can be deformed, disfigured by this terror. Once fear is exorcised, the mask falls away, and the most repellent child changes unrecognizably.

The ugliest and least ingratiating baby seems transformed as if by a magic wand. The child once seen as monster is revealed as beauty.

No, there are no ugly babies. Only those deformed by fear.

5

"Are the specifics of birth so very important?" some will ask.

Birth is only a brief moment, they will say, a mere flash between the long "before" of pregnancy, and the even longer "after" of growing up.

"So if the newborn baby cries while it's arriving, does it really matter?" It's a bad moment to go through, but why make such a fuss about it?

A bad moment to go through . . . all too easy to dismiss it. And yet there's another "bad moment"—just as brief—which nevertheless casts its great shadow over our entire lives. The moment of death.

Yes, both take only a mere moment.

But a moment unlike any other.

To be born is to breathe. To commence this ebb and flow that will cease only when we do.

Our breathing is the fragile vessel that carries us from birth to death.

Everything that lives, breathes.

Every human being breathes.

But how?

Whether respiration is free or impaired makes all the difference. How many people go through life half-strangled! Incapable of even a real sigh, much less a real laugh!

To live freely is to breathe freely. Not with the shoulders or the chest but with the abdomen, with the sides, with the back.

To live—to breathe—fully, requires a straight back, a free spinal column. Supple, and live, and flexible.

How many go through life with a broomstick for a spine?

Is it commonly known that the mentally ill are generally incapable of deep inhalation?

That if there is the least blockage along the spine, respiration— life—is impaired? And the person is disabled forever.

Respiration begins at the moment of birth. As do its potential failings.

At that moment, its character is settled forever.

Just as no two people have the same face, there are no two identical patterns of breathing. Every human being breathes in his own way. Most of the time badly.

Many people acknowledge this when they say: "I'm not breathing right, I must learn how."

There are even those who try to learn.

To learn to breathe!

But your way of breathing was established—once and for all—at the moment you were born.

Later is too late. It was at that exact instant that it had to be dealt with.

6

Others say, more seriously: "Doubtless birth does mark the child, but life is no game. It's a merciless battle. A jungle. So, like it or not, aggression is essential."

It is a total error to imagine that birth without violence breeds children who are passive, weak, numb. Just the contrary.

Birth without violence breeds children who are strong, because they are free, without conflict. Free and fully awake.

Aggression is not strength. It is exactly the opposite.

Aggression and violence are the masks of weakness, impotence, and fear.

Strength is sure, sovereign, smiling.

But I'm afraid I'll have a hard time convincing the advocates of aggression. They themselves have suffered, and so they say: "Life has been hard for me. I've been knocked around, and it's made me what I am. Let it be the same for my children."

Really what they are saying, without admitting it, is: "I've suffered. Why shouldn't others suffer too?"

The dreadful law of reprisal.

These are the same people who used to say (or who even now still say): "Women suffer in childbirth. All right, that must be because they have to."

This is frightful, *a posteriori* logic. We know what people really mean by all the "It must be's" of this kind. They are really talking about evil, sin, and atonement. The cult of suffering isn't new with us. It leads directly back to the stake, to the Inquisition, to all the massacres committed in the name of King or conscience.

There is no sin involved here.

There is only error and ignorance. Our blindness and our resignation.

This kind of suffering is without point. It serves no purpose. It satisfies no God. It springs from a failure of intelligence.

Natural childbirth—childbirth without pain—stands as proof of this.

7

At the end of our tale, I can say only one thing: "Try."

Everything that has been said here is simple. So simple that one feels ashamed to be so insistent about it.

Perhaps we have lost our taste for the simple.

Yes, so few things are essential. None of these costly gadgets for monitoring, none of the other things that are the pride of our technology and are so in fashion now.

None of them.

Only a little patience and humility. A little silence. Unobtrusive but real attention. Awareness of the newcomer as a person. Unself-consciousness.

And love is necessary too.

Without love, the delivery room can be perfect—lighted only as strongly as necessary, the walls soundproofed, the bath temperature at just the right degree—and still the child will howl.

If there's still some vestige of nervousness in you, some ill humor or impatience, some suppressed anger, the baby won't fail to sense it.

The baby has a miraculous sureness in understanding us.

The baby knows everything. *Feels* everything.

The baby sees into the bottom of our hearts, knows the color of our thoughts.

All without language.

The newborn baby is a mirror, reflecting our image. It is for us to make its entrance into the world a joy.

8

"You forgot something."

"What?"

"These children, born in silence and love—what becomes of them? Are they different from the others?"

"It's hard to say. You have to see them."

"And...?"

"Do you remember we said that when the baby is born it wears a mask which hides it, disfigures it, makes it ugly: the mask of trag-edy—brows knitted, corners of the mouth turned down. But then there is another mask. A mask of gaiety, of joy—a mask of comedy.

With a mouth that's relaxed and the corners of the lips lifted in a smile. With eyebrows relaxed too, and eyes crinkled with pleasure..."

"But surely *that* mask has never been seen on a newborn baby! It's impossible."

"You think so? Look..."

"Oh! That baby isn't smiling—it's *laughing!* It's bursting out laughing!"

"It's you yourself who say so."

"How marvelous...But this has nothing to do with what we've been discussing."

"And why not?"

"We've been discussing birth and newborn babies. You're showing me a child six months old."

"Six months old?"

"Infants don't smile before two months. One and a half at the earliest. As for laughing aloud..."

"That's what people say. But *this* baby isn't even twenty-four hours old!"

"I can't believe it!"

"I admit it doesn't happen very often, at least not yet. But...do you know that there's still another mask? Or rather a *real* face without any mask at all?"

"I don't understand."

"Our emotions are states of mind—impermanent, always changing. We cherish certain of them, others we fear. But in reality they are all one. Laughter and tears are very close to one another. And this great joy which so astonishes you in one baby is ultimately no more remarkable than another baby's sorrow. It is still only a mask."

"But what can be left when the child is *without* a mask? What is there when both pain and joy have disappeared? Is there nothing at all?"

"Almost nothing. Yet look..."

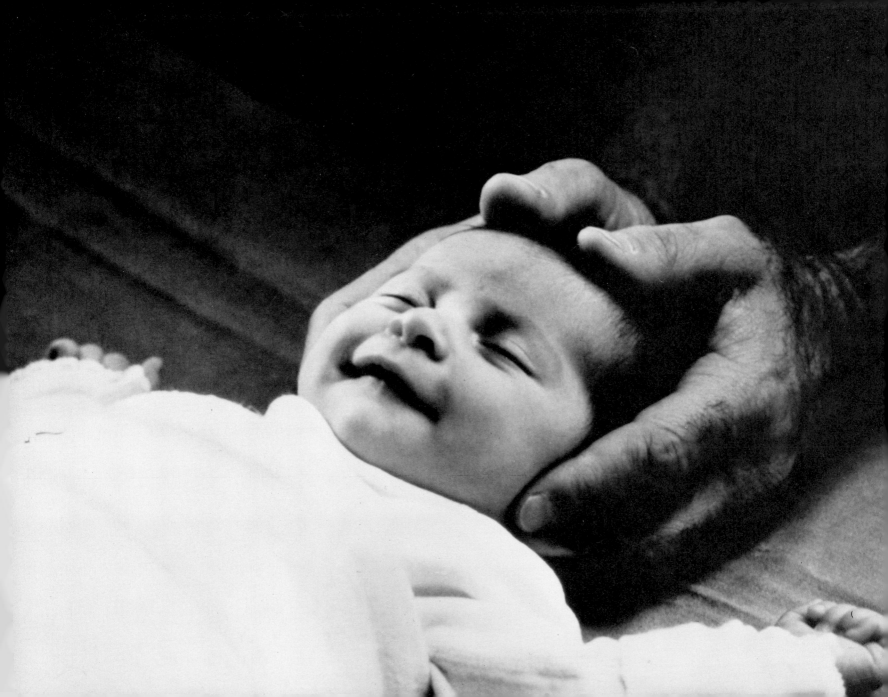

A Note About the Type

The text of this book was set in a film version of Optima,
a typeface designed by Hermann Zapf from 1952-55 and issued in 1958.
In designing Optima, Zapf created a truly new type form—a cross
between the classic roman and a sans-serif face. So delicate are
the stresses and balances in Optima that it rivals sans-serif faces
in clarity and freshness and old-style faces in variety and interest.

Text composed by TypoGraphic Innovations, Inc., New York, New York.
Display set by Haber Typographers Inc., New York, New York.
Printed by Halliday Lithograph Corporation, West Hanover, Massachusetts.
Bound by Economy Bookbinding Corporation, Kearny, New Jersey.
Designed by Betty Anderson.

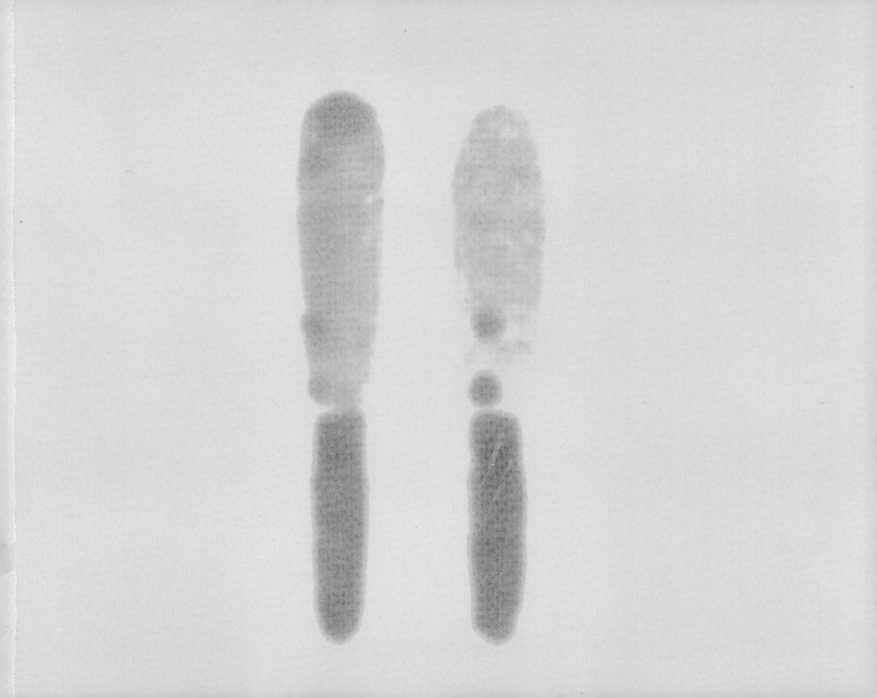